CONTENTS

Abbreviations and Acronyms		2
Introduction: Escalation		2
1	Opposing Forces	5
2	The Battlefield	18
3	Opening Moves	19
4	Assaults on Chernihiv	25
5	The Bypass Attempt	31
6	The Siege	38
7	Radioactive Vacation	47
8	Subversive and Guerrilla Operations	51
9	Russian Withdrawal	54
10	Consequences	57
Bibliography		61
Endnotes		61
About the Author		64

Helion & Company Limited
Unit 8 Amherst Business Centre
Budbrooke Road
Warwick
CV34 5WE
England
Tel. 01926 499 619
Email: info@helion.co.uk
Website: www.helion.co.uk
Twitter: @helionbooks
https://helionbooks.wordpress.com/

Text © Mikhail Zhirokhov 2025
Photographs © as individually credited
Artworks: Giorgio Albertini, David Bocquelet, Luca Canossa, Tom Cooper, Goran Sudar
Maps: Tom Cooper

Cover image: A Russian BTR-82A destroyed in the fighting around Chernihiv in spring 2022. (Maksym Blakitniy via M.Zhirohov)

Designed and typeset by Mach 3 Solutions (www.mach3solutions.co.uk)
Cover design Paul Hewitt, Battlefield Design (www.battlefield-design.co.uk)

Every reasonable effort has been made to trace copyright holders and to obtain their permission for the use of copyright material. The author and publisher apologise for any errors or omissions in this work, and would be grateful if notified of any corrections that should be incorporated in future reprints or editions of this book.

ISBN: 978-1-804519-67-7

British Library Cataloguing-in-Publication Data
A catalogue record for this book is available from the British Library

All rights reserved. No part of this publication may be reproduced, stored in a retrieval system, or transmitted, in any form, or by any means, electronic, mechanical, photocopying, recording or otherwise, without the express written consent of Helion & Company Limited.

We always welcome receiving book proposals from prospective authors.

MAP OF EUROPE SINCE 1992

Note: In order to simplify the use of this book, all names, locations and geographic designations are as provided in *The Times World Atlas*, or other traditionally accepted major sources of reference, as of the time of described events.

ABBREVIATIONS AND ACRONYMS

AB	air base
ASCC	Air Standardisation Coordinating Committee
ATGM	anti-tank guided missile
ATO	Anti-Terrorist Operation
BTG	battalion tactical group
CAA	Combined Arms Army
CBRN	chemical, biological, radiological, and nuclear (formerly referred to as NBC/nuclear, biological, chemical)
ERA	explosive reactive armour
GCAA	Guards Combined Arms Army
GMRB	Guards Motor Rifle Brigade
GUR	*Holovne upravlinnia rozvidky Ministerstva oborony Ukrainy* (Main Directorate of Intelligence of the Ministry of Defence of Ukraine)
GRU	*Glavnoye Razvedyatelnoye Upravleniye*, Main Intelligence (Directorate of the General Staff of the Armed Forces of the Russian Federation; formerly the Main Intelligence Directorate, still colloquially referred to by its old abbreviation)
HQ	headquarters
IFV	infantry fighting vehicle
KGB	*Komitet Gosudarstvennoy Bezopasnosti* (State Security Committee, the main security agency of the Soviet Union)
MANPAD	man-portable air defence (system)
MBT	main battle tank
MiG	Mikoyan i Gurevich (the design bureau led by Artyom Ivanovich Mikoyan and Mikhail Iosifovich Gurevich, also known as OKB-155 or MMZ 'Zenit')
MLRS	multiple launch rocket system (also referred to as multiple rocket launchers)
MRB	Motor Rifle Brigade
NATO	North Atlantic Treaty Organization
NPP	nuclear power plant
OSK	*Ob'edinjonnoe strategicheskoe komandovanie* (Strategic Operational Command) (Russia)
SPH	self-propelled howitzer
SSO	*Sili special'nih operacij Zbrojnih sil Ukraïni* (Special Operations Forces of the Armed Forces of Ukraine)
UAV	Unmanned Aerial Vehicle
USSR	Union of Soviet Socialist Republics
VKS	*Vozdushno-kosmicheskie sily* (Russian Air and Space Forces)
VSRF	*Vooruzhonnije Síly Rossíyskoj Federátsii* (Armed Forces of the Russian Federation)
Yak	Yakovlev (the design bureau led by Alexander Yakovlev, also known as OKB-115 or MMZ 'Skorost')
ZSU	*Zbroiynyh syl Ukrayiny* (Armed Forces of Ukraine)

INTRODUCTION: ESCALATION

The Russian-Ukrainian War that began in the spring of 2014 with the annexation of Crimea, turned into a full-scale invasion by the Armed Forces of the Russian Federation (VSRF) on 24 February 2022. One of the areas of attack was the northern-eastern part of Ukraine, primarily Chernihiv Oblast, which the Russian generals saw as an easy target and one of the springboards for capturing the country's capital, Kyiv. However, in the end, for more than a month, the Russians failed to realise their plans. Therefore, the history of the defence of Chernihiv region in general and Chernihiv in particular is quite symptomatic for what happened early during this war.

As of 2021, hostilities in Donbas, which had been ongoing since April 2014, were frozen by the signing of the so-called Minsk agreements (in September 2014 and February 2015). Although Russia managed to present itself as a non-party to the conflict, it failed to force Ukraine to hold direct talks with representatives of the Donetsk and Luhansk 'republics'. For Kyiv, such negotiations were unacceptable, as they would de facto mean recognising these puppet entities and relinquishing sovereignty over these territories. The spring 2019 elections, which resulted in the election of Volodymyr Zelenskyy as president of Ukraine, gave rise to hopes among Russians that the Ukrainian side would make concessions. After all, one of the slogans of the future president's election campaign was to end the war. However, these hopes were not realised.

Therefore, in 2021, Russia set out to escalate tensions, hoping to force Ukraine to make concessions. Thus, on 3 March 2021, the militants of the self-proclaimed Donetsk People's Republic announced that they had received permission to use 'pre-emptive fire to destroy' the positions of the Armed Forces of Ukraine. Leonid Kravchuk, head of the Ukrainian delegation to the Trilateral Contact Group for the Settlement of the Situation in Donbas, called such statements a violation of the Minsk agreements. At the same time, the shelling of Ukrainian positions, which resulted in the deaths of Ukrainian soldiers, has become much more frequent.

Against this backdrop, Russia began to deploy troops to Ukraine's border in the spring, citing preparations for the Zapad 2021 (West 2021) exercise, even though the exercise itself was scheduled for September. In general, it is a typical practice for Russians to disguise preparations for an invasion with military exercises. Let us recall, for example, the five-day war with Georgia in August, which was preceded by the large-scale Caucasus 2008 exercises. The joint Russian-Belarusian exercises Zapad 2021 were supposed to be unprecedented in scale. On 30 March 2021, the then Commander-in-Chief of the Armed Forces of Ukraine, Colonel General Ruslan Khomchak, said that 28 Russian battalion tactical groups (BTGs) had already been deployed along the border with Ukraine in Rostov, Bryansk, Voronezh regions, as well as in the occupied Crimea.

The escalation moved from land to airspace, where Russian helicopters began to intrude into Ukrainian airspace, and to the sea. Russia deployed additional boats from the Caspian flotilla to the Sea of Azov. On the night from 14 to 15 April, an incident occurred in the Sea of Azov between three Ukrainian boats escorting civilian vessels and six Russian Coast Guard ships and boats. It did not come to the use of weapons, but on 15 April Russia announced that from the following week until October 2021, it would close a part of the Black Sea in the direction of the Kerch Strait to warships and government vessels from other countries under the pretext of military exercises.

Russian and Belarusian troops at the opening of the Zapad 2021 exercises. (MoD Russian Federation)

This was a gross violation of the right to freedom of navigation guaranteed by the UN Convention on the Law of the Sea.

According to the US Department of Defense, as of 20 April 2021, Russia had already concentrated more troops along the border with Ukraine than in 2014. However, the Russian leadership had so far decided not to resort to an open invasion. Russian Defence Minister Sergei Shoigu said that the 'combat readiness check' of the troops of the Southern and Western Military Districts was completed and that starting from 23 April, the military units would return to their permanent locations.

The military and political leadership of Ukraine took certain measures in response to the growing Russian threat: the formation of Territorial Defence forces was accelerated, anti-sabotage exercises were conducted, and so on. However, the most important were the personnel changes in the top leadership of the Armed Forces. On 27 July 2021, Major General (Lieutenant General from 24 August 2021, and General from 4 March 2022) Valeriy Zaluzhnyi became Commander-in-Chief of the Armed Forces of Ukraine. The next day, Major General (Lieutenant General from 24 August 2021) Serhiy Shaptala was appointed Chief of the General Staff of the Armed Forces of Ukraine. Both of them were officers of the new formation, whose careers had been built since Ukraine's independence. Both received good military education and had extensive military experience. For example, Valeriy Zaluzhnyi commanded Sector C in the ATO (Anti-Terrorist Operation) since July 2014 (this sector covered the northern districts of Donetsk and western districts of Luhansk regions). Shaptala, still in the rank of colonel, commanded the 128th Mountain Infantry Brigade in 2014–2017 and took part in the battles for Debaltseve, and on 18 February 2015 he was awarded the title of Hero of Ukraine. Probably, no more-suitable candidates could have been chosen to prepare the Armed Forces of Ukraine for a major war than these two officers.[1]

Generals Valeriy Zaluzhnyi (right) and Serhiy Shaptala. (ZSU)

Meanwhile, Russia continued to prepare for the invasion. Politically, Putin managed to achieve complete subordination of Belarus, led by dictator Alexander Lukashenko. The Ukraine's 'quiet' northern border was thus instantly converted into a potential front line. This was confirmed by the joint Russian-Belarusian exercise Zapad 2021, the largest military exercise in Europe since the collapse of the Union of Soviet Socialist Republics (USSR). Held from 10 to 15 September 2021 at nine training grounds in Russia and five in Belarus, as well as in the Baltic Sea, this involved – according to official figures – about 200,000 military personnel. According to official releases from the General Staff in Moscow, the exercises practiced conducting a defensive operation with a transition to a counteroffensive: repelling an enemy attack, drawing them into 'cauldrons', encircling them, destroying them, and then going on the offensive. The first stage (repulsing the enemy attack) is similar to what Russian troops tried to do after the start of the full-scale invasion of Ukraine. In addition, the exercises provided an excuse and an opportunity to deploy significant forces to the border with Ukraine.

The relative calm on the front line in Donbas lasted until late October and early November, when mutual attacks resumed. According to OSCE observers, the ceasefire was violated twice as often as in 2020 (between the evening of 29 October and the evening of 31 October, the ceasefire was violated 988 times in Donetsk region and 471 times in Luhansk region). This was again accompanied by an increase in diplomatic activity, often in unprecedented forms. For example, on 2–3 November, CIA Director William Burns visited Moscow. In talks with Russian intelligence leaders, he conveyed to the Kremlin US President Joe Biden's concern about the situation on the border with Ukraine. But Russia continued its military preparations. In early November, this process led US authorities to warn the EU that Russia might be planning an invasion of Ukraine. The reaction of the Russian authorities to these signals was predictable. Russian presidential spokesman Dmitry Peskov denied the accusations against Russia, saying instead that it was Ukraine that was 'planning aggressive actions against Donbas'. He also called on the North Atlantic Treaty Organization (NATO) to stop 'concentrating its military fist' near Russia's borders and to stop arming Ukraine with modern weapons. And the Chief of the General Staff of the Russian Armed Forces, Valery Gerasimov, said that the supply of weapons to Ukraine, '…pushes the Ukrainian authorities to take drastic and dangerous steps. Any provocations by the Ukrainian authorities through the forced settlement of the Donbas problems will be suppressed'.

The position of the Ukrainian authorities gradually changed. In early November 2021, Ukrainian intelligence claimed that information about the deployment of additional Russian troops to the Ukrainian border was nothing more than 'an element of psychological pressure'. However, a week later, the Office of the President of Ukraine admitted that the Russian Federation was reinforcing 'specific groups of troops' near the border. Ukraine's Foreign Minister Dmytro Kuleba called on the governments of France and Germany to prepare for a possible military scenario of Russia's actions in the Ukrainian direction. On 3 December, Ukrainian Defence Minister Oleksiy Reznikov, speaking to members of the Verkhovna Rada, said: 'There is a possibility of a large-scale escalation on the part of Russia. The most likely time to achieve readiness for escalation will be the end of January'. His statement was confirmed by foreign analysts. Additional Russian forces arrived in Crimea, and in mid-January 2022, there were reports of Russian military units arriving in Belarus under the pretext of preparing for the next joint exercises scheduled for February.

All attempts at a diplomatic settlement of the conflict had failed. Russia stubbornly put forward unacceptable demands, such as providing legal guarantees of NATO's non-expansion to the east, abandoning the 2008 Bucharest Summit decisions that Ukraine and Georgia would become NATO members, and legally enshrining a ban on the deployment of strike weapons systems that posed a

Airborne troops were key to the 2022 rush, according to Russian generals. (MoD Russian Federation)

Exercise Allied Resolve 2022 was the final Russian preparation for an invasion of Ukraine. (Russian MOD)

threat to Russia on the territory of its neighbouring countries by the United States and other NATO countries. At the same time, the Russian leadership demonstratively refused to negotiate with Ukraine, insisting on direct contacts with the United States, saying that 'one should talk to the master, not the servant'. It was becoming clear that the Russian leadership was headed for war. Under these circumstances, in mid-January, the West (the United States, the United Kingdom, and later the Baltic states, Poland, and others) began providing Ukraine with emergency military assistance. Initially, this consisted of light infantry weapons that were easy for personnel to use but effective in close combat: anti-tank guided missiles (ATGMs), grenade launchers, man-portable air defence systems (MANPADS).

The immediate prelude to the Russian invasion was the Russian-Belarusian exercise Allied Resolve 2022 held from 10 to 20 February 2022. It is noteworthy that the number of troops participating in them was not officially announced. To participate in them, units of the Russian Eastern Military District were deployed to Belarus, including aviation (with Su-35S fighters and Su-25SM attack aircraft) and air defence (two S-400 and one Pantsir-S1 air defence systems).

Episodes of the Allied Resolve 2022 exercise took place in other areas, including the Black Sea, in addition to the territory of Belarus. Under this pretext, the Russians blocked a large part of the Black and Azov Seas, making it impossible for ships from Berdyansk and Mariupol to enter the Black Sea.

Meanwhile, the media began to report the dates of the expected Russian attack. Western countries one after another recommended that their citizens leave Ukraine, and foreign airlines stopped flying to Ukraine. The last diplomatic chord was struck at the Munich Security Conference, which took place on 18–20 February. President Zelensky attended, despite the White House's concern that Russia might attack while the president was away. As we know, this did not happen. There were unanimous statements of support for Ukraine at the conference. However, there was no dialog; Russia ignored the Munich Conference for the first time since 1999. The Great War became inevitable.

1

OPPOSING FORCES

During the Battle of Chernihiv, both Russia and Ukraine deployed relatively different combat formations. Many of these came into being on the basis of ages-old military traditions; others had unusual composition or equipment. This chapter provides a closer look at the principal formations from both sides.

Ukrainian Forces

As of February 2022, very few units of the Armed Forces of Ukraine were based in the Chernihiv region, and all forces were concentrated in three settlements: Chernihiv, Honcharivske and Desna. Elements of the National Guard and a fairly large group of the State Border Guard Service were deployed along the border, while the Territorial Defence was mobilised only at the outbreak of active hostilities.

1st Separate 'Severskaya' Tank Brigade

Established in 1997 from the former 292nd Tank Regiment of the 72nd Motor Rifle Division and the 280th Tank Regiment of the 25th Motor Rifle Division of the Soviet Army, the 1st Tank Brigade took over the battle flag of the 292nd Tank Regiment, its military orders and historical form, and was home-based in Honcharivske. The latter was a town founded in 1953 as a military facility under the authority of the Kiev Military District. At the same time, a training ground was created nearby. The reconnaissance of the exact location of the settlement, as well as the training ground, was especially carried out by the commander of the Kiev Military District, Army General Vasil Ivanovich Chuikov, who was the initiator of this creation. Until 1986, Honcharivske grew into a military city, housing 18 different units, including mechanised, tank, artillery, missile, engineering,

Home-base of the 1st Separate Tank Brigade in Honcharivske. (Ukrainian MOD)

aviators and paratroopers. At one time, Honcharivske was planned to become a military town for the military training of armies of the Warsaw Pact countries.

The process of working up the 1st Tank Brigade developed smoothly, as both of its original regiments were stationed at the same facility. Initially, they were equipped with a total of 101 T-64 tanks, 14 BMP-2 infantry fighting vehicles (IFVs), two BMP-1 IFVs, three BMP-1KSHs, two PRP-3s, four BRM-1Ks, 24 2S1 Gvozdika self-propelled howitzers (SPHs), as well as two MT-55A and 29 MT-LB armoured engineering vehicles. Certainly enough, not all of this equipment was retained when the 1st Tank was reorganised into three battalions, but the brigade was renowned as one of the best in terms of training and maintaining combat readiness even at the times the Ukrainian armed forces were in terrible condition, during the late 1990s, and for most of the 2010s. Thus, in 2000, the 1st Tank was awarded the title of the 1st Guards Separate Novgorod Tank Brigade of the Orders of the Red Banner, Bohdan Khmelnitsky, Kutuzov, Alexander Nevsky, and the Red Star.

Starting in 1999, the command and personnel proposed that the brigade be given the name *Chernihiv*. Eventually, they limited themselves to adding Novhorod-Chernihiv to the name. Ironically, the 1st Tank thus went into the war in Donbas still wearing the old Soviet title 'Guards': this was removed by decree by President Petro Poroshenko only on 22 August 2016. Instead, a year later, on 23 August 2017, the brigade was given the honorary name *Siverskaya*, after the historical region Severshchina, in present-day southwest Russia, northern Ukraine and eastern Belarus, the central part of which was the city of Chernihiv.

Given its high level of training and combat readiness, the 1st Tank was the first unit of the *Zbroiynyh syl Ukrayiny* (Armed Forces of Ukraine, ZSU) to receive the most modern main battle tank (MBT) of Ukraine: the T-64BM Bulat. Designed in the mid-1990s by designers from Kharkiv, the Bulat was the T-64BV with Nozh explosive reactive armour (ERA), a guided missile system and the 1A45 fire control system (as installed on much more modern Russian MBTs like the T-80UD and T-84), and the 6EC43 auto-loader.[1]

Originally, the Ministry of Defence in Kyiv planned to upgrade the entire fleet of 400 T-64B/BVs to the T-64BM standard. However, due to lack of funding and political will, in 2004 the military's appetite was cut back and only 85 tanks were funded for modernisation. At that time, the total cost of modernisation of one vehicle was estimated at a mere US$500,000. By the beginning of 2009, the state had purchased a total of 56 tanks, all of which were assigned to the 1st Tank. Then an additional contract was signed for 29 tanks: the first 10 of these were handed over to the Ministry of Defence, and thus to the unit, on 28 October 2010. Ten additional T-64BMs arrived in Honcharivske by the end of 2011: the last nine were scheduled for delivery in early 2012, but actually reached the 1st Tank only shortly before it was deployed for the ATO in Donbas, on 28 March 2014, and even then they lacked the ERA.

In contrast to the 17th Separate Tank Brigade, as of spring 2014, the 1st Tank Brigade thus had all of its nominally assigned tanks. Its 1st and 3rd Battalions were equipped with a total of 82 T-64BM Bulats, while the 2nd Battalion operated a total of 43 of different earlier sub-variants, including T-64Bs, T-64BM2s, and T-64BVs.

Additionally, Honcharivske was now a storage site for a large number of vehicles from numerous disbanded units, foremost the 128th Independent Mountain Infantry Brigade. In late 2014, this enabled the establishment of two independent tank battalions at the 169th Desna Training Centre: these greatly helped compensate losses of the 1st Tank during the war in Donbas.

Following the Russian occupation of Crimea and the beginning of the ATO, the brigade was urgently reinforced through addition of mobilised soldiers, mostly natives of the Chernihiv region. Unlike other brigades, no battalion tactical groups were formed on the basis of the 1st Tank Brigade. The only mechanised battalion on BMP-1 IFVs was divided into three companies, each of which was reinforced by a tank company, thus essentially becoming improvised company tactical groups. A brigade artillery group was also formed with self-

Arrival of new T-64BM Bulat tanks. (Author's collection)

Tankers of the 1st Tank brigade in the zone of ATO, Donbas. (Author's collection)

propelled howitzers and BM-21 multiple launch rocket systems (MLRS), which was used as a fire reinforcement at the disposal of the Sector A headquarters. In addition, during the defence of the Luhansk airport in the summer of 2014, a consolidated group acted virtually autonomously.

In 2014–2015, the 1st Tank Brigade took part in the Battle for Luhansk, the Battle for Donetsk Airport, and fought in the Battle of Debaltseve. Subsequently, it continued serving in Donbas on rotational basis until 2021. A total of 55 of its officers and 239 non-commissioned officers were decorated for bravery and other achievements.[2] Through this period, its composition and equipment continued to change. For example, in spring of 2017, T-64BMs were transferred to a reservist formation and replaced by T-64BV Model 2017s. Correspondingly, as of February 2022, the 1st Tank Brigade was organised as shown in Table 1.

Table 1: Organisation of 1st Tank Brigade in February 2022

Brigade Headquarters	
1st Tank Battalion	equipped with T-64BV tanks
2nd Tank Battalion	equipped with T-64BV tanks
3rd Tank Battalion	equipped with T-64BV tanks
Mechanised Battalion	equipped with BMP-1 IFV
Artillery Group, including:	
1st Artillery Division	self-propelled artillery, equipped with 2S1 Gvozdika (122mm)
2nd Artillery Division	self-propelled artillery, equipped with 2S3 Akatsiya (152mm)
3rd Artillery Division	rocket artillery, equipped with BM-21 Grad MLRS
Anti-Aircraft Defence Battalion	equipped with 9K38 Igla MANPADs infrared homing surface-to-air missile system (ASCC/NATO reporting name 'SA-18 Grouse'), 9K35 Strela-10 short-range surface-to-air missile system ('SA-13 Gopher') and 2K22 Tunguska tracked self-propelled anti-aircraft gun self-propelled anti-aircraft systems ('SA-19 Grisom')
Reconnaissance Company	
Engineer Battalion	equipped with UR-77 Meteorit mine-clearing vehicles and GMZ-series minelayers[3]
Logistic Battalion	
Maintenance Battalion	
Signals Company	
Radar Company	
Medical Company	

58th Independent Motorized Infantry Brigade 'Hetman Ivan Vyhovskyi'

The second major ZSU unit to become involved in the Battle of Chernihiv was not deployed directly inside the city. The 58th Motorised Brigade was established on 17 February 2015 in Sumy and took command over three battalions of the Territorial Defence, consisting of volunteers:

- 13th (former Chernihiv-1 Territorial Defence battalion)
- 15th (former Sumi Territorial Defence battalion)
- 16th (former Poltava Territorial Defence battalion)

Since 2016, the headquarters of the brigade were in Konotop, and the unit then fought in Donbass near Avdiivka (Donetsk region) and in Bakhmutka (Lugansk region). On 6 May 2019, at the first celebration of Infantry Day, the brigade received the honorary name *Hetman Ivan Vyhovsky*.[4] As of February 2022, the 58th Motorised Brigade was organised as shown in Table 2.

Table 2: Organisation of 58th Motorised Brigade in February 2022

Brigade HQ	
13th Motorized Battalion	based in Voronizh, Sumy Oblast, equipped with BMP-1 IFV
15th Motorized Battalion	based in Stetskivka, Sumy Oblast, equipped with BMP-1 IFV
16th Motorized Battalion	based in Hlukiv, Sumy Oblast, equipped with BMP-1 IFV
Tank Battalion	equipped with T-64BV tanks
Artillery Group, including	
1st Artillery Division	towed artillery, equipped with gun-howitzer D-20 (152 mm)
2nd Artillery Division	self-propelled artillery, equipped with 2S1 Gvozdika (122mm)
3rd Artillery Division	rocket artillery, equipped with BM-21 Grad MLRS
Anti-Aircraft Defence Battalion	equipped with Igla MANPADs, Strela-10 short-range surface-to-air missile system
Reconnaissance Company	
Engineer Battalion	
Logistic Battalion	
Maintenance Battalion	
Signals Company	
Radar Company	
Medical Company	
CBRN Protection Company	

Other ZSU Units

Additional units that took part in the fighting in Chernihiv were:

12th Independent Tank Battalion

The 12th Independent Tank Battalion, ZSU, was established in 2019, and equipped with T-64BM Bulat tanks from the 1st Tank Brigade, as well as a few additional vehicles from reserve weapons depots. Subsequently, the unit was trained and tasked with protection of the northern part of Chernihiv Oblast, in cooperation with the 61st Jäger Infantry Brigade.[5]

Regional Centre for Radio-Electronic Intelligence North

Established on 1 December 1991 as the 68th Independent Special Purpose Radio-Engineering Regiment of the Soviet Army, in 2005, this unit was reformed into the Regional Centre of Radio-Electronic Intelligence North. Its purpose was to conduct radio-electronic reconnaissance. Since the first days of the ATO, the staff of the Regional Centre for Radio-Electronic Intelligence North had been involved in all operations in the Donbas. Tasks were performed both at the point of permanent deployment and through rotation. The Centre thus passed almost the entire front line of the ATO, from Stanytsia Luhanska, Luhansk Oblast, to Mariupol, Donetsk Oblast. The unit was also involved in peacekeeping operations and performed other tasks.[6]

Soldiers of the 13th Territorial Defence Battalion "Chernihiv-1", summer 2014. (Author's collection)

T-64BVs from the tank battalion of the 58th Motorised Brigade. (Ukrainian MOD)

5th Independent Communications Regiment
Established in 2015, over the following year the Regiment performed tasks in the Donetsk and Luhansk regions, with numerous of its officers and other ranks earning themselves high state awards.[7]

134th Security & Service Battalion Operational Command North
Established in March 2015, in Chernihiv.

169th Training Centre Desna
The current training centre dates back to 1 December 1987, when the 48th Training Division of the Soviet Army was reorganised as the 169th District Training Centre, and adjusted to provide training for junior specialists of tank forces. Alongside this came the construction of the urban settlement of Desna.

In 1992, the training centre became one of the first Ukrainian units whose personnel took the oath of allegiance to the people of

A Second World War vintage IS-3 tank on a pedestal at the entrance to the 169th Desna Training Centre. (Ukrainian MOD)

Ukraine. At that time, the 169th Guards District Training Centre of the Kyiv Military District had 240 tanks (233 T-64s, seven T-55s), 232 IFVs (130 BMP-2s, 98 BMP-1s, four BRM-1Ks), 13 armoured personnel carriers (nine BTR-70s, four BTR-60s), 54 SPH (18 2S1 Gvozdika, 36 2S3 Akatsiya), 12 guns (nine D-30s, three M-30s), 19 mortars (14 2S12 Sani, five PM-38), as well as eight MLRS (seven BM-21, one BM-13).

In 1992–2000 the training centre included six regiments: three training tank regiments (5th, 300th and 389th), training motorized rifle regiment (354th), artillery training regiment (467th) and a training anti-aircraft missile regiment (1121st). In addition, organizationally, it included seven independent educational battalions. On 30 June 2000 the connection was reformatted into the 169th Training Centre of the Ground Forces Ukraine, which officially became known as Desna. Amid the general process of downsizing of the Ukrainian armed forces, in 2011, the Desna was reduced to four training regiments and two independent training battalions.

119th Independent Brigade of the Territorial Defence

The 119th Independent Brigade of the Territorial Defence was established on 29 March 2018, following a joint directive of the Ministry of Defence of Ukraine and the General Staff of the Armed Forces of Ukraine, and the directive of the commander of the Operational Command North.

As of 24 February 2022, the brigade was commanded by Colonel Oleksiy Vysotskyi, and 80 percent manned but still in peacetime status. Early that morning, the brigade was mobilised and instantly put on alert for deploying in reaction to the Russian invasion: a task that had to be accomplished while its base was subjected to repeated Russian missile and artillery rocket strikes, and, later on, while the unit was effectively surrounded. Immediately after receiving weapons, personnel moved to designated positions in order to defend the perimeter of Chernihiv and prevent the city from being captured by the enemy. Of the available six battalions, four were deployed for the defence of Chernihiv, while one battalion each participated in the defence of Nizhyn and Pryluky. Combat operations of the brigade's elements were conducted in cooperation with other units of the Armed Forces of Ukraine, Special Operations Forces (SSO), the State Border Service of Ukraine, the National Guard of Ukraine, as well as volunteer formations of residents of Chernihiv Oblast.

54th Independent Military Reconnaissance Battalion Mykhailo Tysha

44th Independent Artillery Brigade Hetman Danylo Apostol

Including one battery of 2A65 Msta-B self-propelled 152mm howitzers.

21st Independent Rifle Battalion of the Territorial Defence
Established in February 2022.

National Guard of Ukraine
22nd Battalion of the 27th Independent "Pechersk" Brigade

Border Guards of Ukraine: 105th Border Guards Detachment 'Prince Volodymyr the Great'
Originally based in the German Democratic Republic, the Ukrainian part of the history of this unit began on 1 March 1993, when the former 105th Independent Riga Red Banner Regiment of the Order of the Red Star of the KGB was relocated from Drohobych, Lviv Oblast, to Chernihiv.

The new border guard detachment was formed pursuant to the order of the President of Ukraine Leonid Kravchuk of October 1992. The 105th Detachment was assigned to protect a section of the border within the Chernihiv and Kyiv regions. This is 408.1km (171.2km by land and 236.9km by river), of which 183km is the border with the Russian Federation and 225.1km with the Republic of Belarus.[8] Since both Belarus and Russia were friendly states at the time, the main problems faced by Chernihiv's Border Guards were fighting smuggling and monitoring local residents' compliance with the border zone regime.

The unit took part in the fighting in Donbas in 2014–2015. In accordance with the Decree of the President of Ukraine No. 619/2019 'On the awarding of honorary names to military units of the State Border Guard Service of Ukraine' of 22 August 2019, the 105th Border Guard Detachment of the Northern Regional Directorate of the State Border Guard Service of Ukraine was awarded the honorary name 'named after Prince Volodymyr the Great' and would be referred to as the 105th Border Guard Detachment named after Prince Volodymyr the Great of the Northern Regional Directorate of the State Border Guard Service of Ukraine.

Ukrainian Commanders
The defence of Chernihiv Oblast (as well as the entire northern border of Ukraine) was the responsibility of the Operational Command North of the ZSU. As of February 2022, this was commanded by Major General Viktor Nikolyuk. Responsible for the defence of the city of Chernihiv was Colonel Dmytro Bryzhynsky.

Major General Viktor Nikolyuk. (Ukrainian MOD)

Base of the 105th Squadron Prince Volodymyr the Great of the Ukrainian Border Guards, seen in 2021. (Author's collection)

Viktor Nikoliuk was born on 19 October 1975 in the Kirovohrad region. In 1992, he graduated from the local school and in 1996 from the Kharkiv Guard Higher Command Tank School. In 2007, he graduated from the National University of Defence. During his service in the Armed Forces of Ukraine, he commanded a reconnaissance company, a tank battalion, and a training mechanised regiment. Later on, he served as the chief-of-staff of the 92nd (Independent) Mechanised Brigade, and then as its commander. Since 2014, Nikoliuk served several tours of duty in Donbas,[9] and in 2015 was wounded during the battle of Trykhizbenka. Following recovery, he returned to duty and received several high awards, including the orders of Bohdan Khmelnytsky III degree and Danylo Halytsky. In March 2017, Colonel Viktor Nikoliuk was appointed head of the 169th Desna Training Centre, and in December 2018 he was given general epaulettes. In October 2021, Major General Nikoliuk was appointed the commander of the Operational Command North.[10]

Dmytro Bryzhynskyi was born in June 1980, in Shchors (now Snovsk), in Chernihiv Oblast. In 2001, he graduated with honours from the Kharkiv Institute of Tank Troops, and then pursued the usual peacetime service from position of a platoon commander to the head of Department of Operational Management at the General Staff of the ZSU. As of 2014, Bryzhynsky commanded a company tactical group of the 1st Tank Brigade and in summer of that year fought in the Luhansk Oblast. In March 2019, he was appointed the commander (CO) of the 93rd (Independent) Mechanised Brigade, which subsequently fought in the Avdiivka sector. As of February 2022, he was heading one of the departments of the Operational Command North.[11]

Of the Ukrainian tactical commanders, the most important role was played by Colonel Leonid Alekseyevich Khoda. Born in 1975, he was in command of the 1st Tank Brigade since 2020, and played a crucial role in the defence of Chernihiv. Much less is known about the CO 58th Motorised Brigade, Colonel Dmytro Kashchenko, except that he skilfully manoeuvred all elements of his unit – although these were scattered over a battlefield stretching over 200 kilometres, and that during a battle fought at high tempo – preventing any of them from being surrounded and cut off by rapidly advancing Russians during the critical first three days of the war.

Colonel Dmytro Bryzhynsky. (Ukrainian MOD)

Colonel Leonid Alekseyevvich Khoda, CO 1st Tank Brigade, ZSU, as of 2022. (ZSU)

CHERNIHIV AVIATION SCHOOL (1951 – 1995)

In the times of the USSR, there were two higher military schools for training of fighter pilots on the territory of Ukraine: one in Chernihiv, and the other in Kharkiv. Only the facility in Kharkiv survived the dissolution of the USSR and the emergence of Ukraine, and continued functioning in the form of the National Air Force University of Ukraine. The Chernihiv aviation school was closed in 1995.

After the end of the Second World War, Soviet aviation universities moved from an accelerated to a systematic and clearly organised system of training. In mid-1946, the Yakovlev Yak-11 (Yak-3UTI) trainer fighter was put into serial production, replacing the long-outdated U-2 biplane and the two-seat version of the Polikarpov I-16 fighter (UTI-4) from the 1930s, in flight schools. The adoption of the Yak-11 made it possible to move away from the so-called two-stage pilot training system, when in flight schools it was actually not possible to fully train pilots on high-speed machines that were in service with combat regiments. Therefore, after graduating from college, newly-minted lieutenants in reserve air regiments mastered new technology on two-seat Yak-7V, Yak-9V and Lavochkin La-7UTI trainers.

Such a system significantly slowed down the training process, and the use of two-seat combat fighters as flying simulators was too expensive. At the same time, the Yak-11 was perfectly suited to the new training system in flight schools, allowing their graduates to immediately get into the cockpits of combat aircraft, bypassing the reserve regiment.

The entry into service of jet aircraft required the development of a fundamentally new flight training methodology. Therefore, in 1948, a flight training course for cadets of fighter, attack and bomber aviation schools, as well as a methodological manual for it, was developed and approved. By 1951 the first group of cadets were trained in the technique of piloting the Mikoyan i Gurevich MiG-15 jet fighter at the Kachin Pilot School.

It was for the training of fighter aviation pilots that the directive of the General Staff of the Soviet Army dated 15 February 1951, laid the foundation for the Air Force Military Aviation School, which received the designation '57'. The choice of location was due primarily to the fact that before the Second World War there had been a military school in the city for some time, and a suitable airfield was available outside Chernihiv.

Emblem of ChVVAUL. (Author's collection)

The school received its first aircraft, the Yak-18 training aircraft, on 12 May 1951. And by July 1951, the school's fleet consisted of 22 Yak-18s, 30 Yak-11s, six Po-2s and one Li-2. In the summer, recruitment began for the theoretical battalion, consisting of 19 classroom departments with a two-year training period.

On 18 February 1952, the school received the first MiG-15 jet fighters. They arrived disassembled and were assembled and prepared for flight on the spot. In August 1953, the first graduation of fighter pilots on the MiG-15 jet fighter took place. Of the 126 cadets who came in September 1951, only 90 received lieutenant's shoulder straps. The average flight time of graduates was 115–120 hours, of which 23–25 were on the MiG-15bis. The next graduation of 102 cadets took place in November of the same year. In the second issue the average flight time was higher, up to 150–160 hours, of which 30–35 hours were on the MiG-15bis.

From 1 October 1959, and according to the Order of the Soviet Ministry of Defence, the 57th Aviation School of Air Force Pilots was transformed into the Chernihiv Higher Military Aviation School of Pilots (ChVVAUL) with a four-year training period.

With the transition of the school to a higher level, the requirements for applicants increased significantly. From 1957,

Yak-18 training aircraft, Pivtsi airfield, 1962. (Author's collection)

Cadet of ChVVAUL in the cockpit of MiG-15UTI. (Author's collection)

flight schools began to accept persons from among civilian youth, soldiers and sergeants of conscript service aged 18–21 with secondary education and fit for flight.

At the beginning of 1963, the command of the Soviet Air Force decided to switch to a new training system, when the main machine with which cadets would transfer to the new generation MiG-21 jet fighters would be the Czechoslovak-made L-29 Dolphin jet training aircraft (the first such an aircraft entered the school on 29 May 1963).

In September 1963, the school graduated its first class of pilot engineers. Among them was the future Soviet cosmonaut Leonid Kizim (1941–2010).

Almost immediately after the development of the Dolphin, the accelerated development of the next generation fighter began; the MiG-21F, MiG-21F-13 and the MiG-21U combat trainer. In 1973, to replace the L-29 Dolphin, the more modern L-39 Albatros was adopted into service at aviation schools of the Soviet Air Force.

In the 1970s, progress moved at a tremendous pace and in May 1976 the school received a new task, to begin training cadets for the third generation MiG-23 fighter. Between 1974 and 1980, the school graduated seven courses of new MiG-23 fighter pilots.

In 1988, training on the MiG-23 aircraft was stopped at ChVVAUL, and in 1990 the last graduation was made on the MiG-21. The school switched to a new flight training system: whereas previously, in three to four flight courses, a cadet mastered two or three types of aircraft (L-29, L-39, MiG-15, MiG-17, MiG-21, MiG-23), and several of their variants, and training in complex types was carried out in combat regiments, then the graduates of 1991–1993 were trained only on L-39 aircraft, but in more complex programs with flights in aerobatics in pairs, combat manoeuvring in pairs, aerobatics at low altitudes, firing S-5/8 rockets at ground targets.

The collapse of the Soviet Union had an extremely negative impact on the work of the school as a whole, although graduations from 1992–1993 were still taking place due to inertia, the Soviet safety margin was still high. This time graduates not only went to combat regiments, but, as a rule, also to different countries.

On 3–5 January 1992, the school's personnel were the first among military universities in Ukraine to take the oath of allegiance to the Ukrainian people. However, later the same year, and against the backdrop of a large-scale reduction in flight personnel, it was decided to disband ChVVAUL. A large number

A MiG-21U at Pivtsi airfield. (Author's collection)

of instructors were sent to the reserve: these were mainly officers that had a sufficient length of service to retire and could be provided with an apartment.

On 30 November 1995 the school was disbanded and a farewell to its banner took place. In turn, effective with 1 November 1995, the 201st Aviation Base began was established from the personnel of the former 701st Training Aviation Regiment. Organizationally, this unit became a part of the Kharkov Institute of Pilots named after Ivan Kozhedub. In 2004, as part of another reorganisation, the 201st Air Base was disbanded, and this is where the history of the unique military university ended. Instead, a military school for enhanced military physical training operated at some of its installation and, from 2014 to 2022, the State Research Institute for Testing and Certification of Weapons and Military Equipment (transferred from the occupied Crimea) was home-based in Chernihiv.

L-39 Albatros from 201st Air Base Ukrainian Air Force, 2001. (Author's collection)

Russian Forces

The precise composition of the VSRF units involved in the invasion of Chernihiv Oblast remains partially unclear – principally because of the destruction of their headquarters (HQ), but also because several units nominally subordinated to the two combined arms armies (CAAs) that entered and operated on the territory of Chernihiv Oblast, were redeployed to other sectors while the battle was still going on. That said, the two CAAs in question had been clearly identified in the days before the fighting began.

In grand total, the VSRF formations that advanced into Chernihiv Oblast comprised about 30,000 officers and other ranks, and 10,000 vehicles: from these, about 15,000 troops and 5,000 vehicles saw direct participation in the Battle of Chernihiv.

Table 3: Chain of command of the Russian forces involved in the invasion of Chernihiv Oblast of Ukraine

Command Node	Headquarters	CO
OSK Centre	Unecha (Bryansk Region, Russian Federation)	Colonel General M. Teplynskyi
OSK Centre Mobile Command Post	Vyshneve (Ukraine)	Colonel General O. P. Lapin
41st CAA	Knevichi (Bryansk Region, Russian Federation)	Major General V. P. Gerasymov
41st CAA Reserve Command Post	Starye Yurkovichi (Bryansk Region, Russian Federation)	
41st CAA Mobile Command Post	Malynivka (Ukraine)	Lieutenant General S. B. Ryzhkov
2nd GCAA	Tetkino (Kursk Region, Russian Federation)	Major General F. M. Bolgarev
2nd GCAA Reserve Command Post	Medvezhye (Russian Federation)	
2nd GCAA Mobile Command Post	Kokhanivka (Ukraine)	Lieutenant General A. V. Kolotovkin

41st Combined Arms Army

Originally worked up in 1942 as the 41st Army, and re-formed to its modern-day status on 1 December 1998 from the former headquarters of the Siberian Military District, the 41st Combined Arms Army was headquartered in Novosibirsk, and subordinated to the Central Military District when, in 2010, the Siberian Military District was disbanded. As of 2022, the 41st CAA nominally included the 35th Motorised Rifle Brigade, the 55th Mountain Motorised Rifle Brigade, the 74th Guards Motorised Rifle Brigade, the 120th Artillery Brigade, the 119th Missile Brigade, and the usual support elements. However, at least parts of nearly all of these units were redeployed to bolster the Russian forces advancing from southern Belarus directly on Kyiv. As a consequence, the 41st CAA launched its part of the invasion in much depleted condition. Its known composition is provided in Table 4.

Table 4: Known units assigned to the 41st CAA, February–early April 2022

Unit	Known number of BTGs	Comment
35th Motor Rifle Brigade	2	
55th Mountain Motor Rifle Brigade		Deployed seemingly with all three manoeuvre battalions
74th Guards Motor Rifle Brigade	2	
90th Guards Tank Division	2	BTGs drawn from the division's 80th Tank Regiment and 228th Motor Rifle Regiment
120th Artillery Brigade	N/A	

35th Independent Motor Rifle Brigade

The traditions of this unit can be traced back to the former 4th Tank Corps, then the 5th Guards Tank Corps, the 5th Guards Tank Division, and then the 122nd Guards Motor Rifle Division of the Soviet Army. That said, the 35th Independent Motor Rifle Brigade was officially established only in June 2009, and headquartered in a former base of the Strategic Rocket Forces, at Aleysk, in Altai Krai. In 2014, the unit was involved in the initial Russian invasion of the Luhansk Oblast in Ukraine. After its involvement in the battles of the Georgievka area, and following the transfer of its T-72BM tanks to pro-Russian paramilitary formations, it was withdrawn back to the Russian Federation and reorganised.

55th Mountain Motor Rifle Brigade

Established in November 2015, the 55th Brigade was headquartered in Kyzyl, in the Tyva Republic of the Russian Federation, and almost entirely staffed by ethnic Tuvans. Trained in mountain warfare, the unit became only the second in the VSRF to deploy horses as pack animals: in total, as of 2019, the brigade had one pack transport company with about 100 horses, but this is not known to have been deployed in Ukraine in 2022. Over the following years, the 55th was additionally equipped with Tigr-M 4x4 multipurpose, all-terrain infantry mobility vehicles, 2S23 Nona-SVK wheeled self-propelled 120mm mortars, Ural heavy trucks and other special equipment and worked up in the course of a number of minor exercises.

74th Guards Motor Rifle Brigade

The 74th Guards Motor Rifle Brigade was established in Yurga, near Tomsk, in the Kemerovo region (at the time in the Siberian Military District), in 1991, through the reorganisation of the 94th Guards Zvenigorod-Berlin Order of Suvorov Motor Rifle Division that was withdrawn from Germany. In 1994–1995, it took part in the First Chechen War, while in 2005 reorganised to be fully staffed by professional soldiers. In 2014, the 74th took part in the annexation of the Crimea and in the summer of the same year was deployed inside Ukraine again: this time in the Luhansk, and then the Donetsk oblasts, where it is known to have taken part in the Ilovaisk operation. The unit remained deployed in Ukraine during the winter of 2014–2015, when its troops operated as the Hooligan Battalion of the so-called Luhansk People's Republic. Later in 2015, elements of the 74th Guards Motor Rifle Brigade were deployed to Syria, while the unit became the first in the Central Military District to be fully re-equipped with T-72B3 MBTs.

120th Artillery Brigade

This unit was headquartered in Chistye Klyuchi, outside Sheekhov, and included three artillery battalions, one of which was equipped with eight BM-27 Uragan MLRS, while two others operated a total of 18 2A65 Msta-B towed 152mm howitzers.

90th Guards Tank Division

Established in 2016, in the Central Military District of the VSRF, through the reorganisation of the 90th Guards Rifle Division, and headquartered in Chebarkul (Chelyabinsk region), the 90th Guards Tank Division inherited a number of regiments and battalions with rich history, including the 6th Guards Lvov Tank Regiment, the 80th Guards Tank Regiment, the 239th Guards Tank Regiment, the 228th Guards Motor Rifle Regiment, the 228th Motor Rifle Regiment, the 400th Guards Self-Propelled Artillery Regiment,

The only photo known to the author of military personnel of the Russian 35th Independent Motorized Rifle Brigade on the territory of the Chernihiv region, spring 2022. (Russian social network Vkontakte)

and the 232nd Guards Rocket Artillery Brigade. The 90th entered the Russian all-out invasion of Ukraine organised into two major parts, one of which saw intensive fighting in Chernihiv Oblast. The part in question included the 80th Tank and the 228th Motor Rifle Regiments, supported by the 400th Self-Propelled Artillery Regiment. Their task was to support the advance of the 41st CAA by quickly driving through the eastern Chernihiv Oblast, crossing the Desna River and then joining the 2nd Guards Combined Arms Army west of the Konotop area, before turning west to push in the Kyiv direction.

2nd Guards Combined Arms Army
Another major formation of the VSRF to take part in the fighting for Chernihiv was the 2nd Guards Combined Arms Army (2nd GCAA), headquartered in Samara. Arguably, the actual task of the 2nd GCAA was to secure the northern Sumy Oblast and then reach Kyiv from the east. Indeed, during the Battle of Chernihiv, in February–March 2022, its major elements remained preoccupied with trying to achieve this aim and thus only minor parts of one of its brigades saw combat in the Chernihiv area. The 2nd GCAA was established in 2001, from the former 2nd Guards Tank Red Banner Army, traditions of which can be traced back to early 1943. Its first command staff exercise took part in 2006, while its primary manoeuvring formations included the 15th, 27th and 30th Guards Motor Rifle Brigades, the 92nd Rocket Brigade, and the 385th Guards Artillery Brigade.

15th Guards Motor Rifle Brigade
The 15th Guards Motor Rifle Brigade came into being on 1 February 2005, through the reorganisation of the 589th Guards Motor Rifle Regiment. Completely staffed by contract personnel, the unit was designed to take part in international peace and security missions under the auspices of the United Nations. Indeed, between late 2005 and until 2008 it carried out the tasks of maintaining peace in the Russian-occupied parts of Georgia. In 2014, elements of the 15th were deployed in the Donbas during the initial Russian invasion of Ukraine, where they took part in the battles near Georgiyivka. The brigade remained in the Luhansk Oblast through 2015 and 2016. In November 2020, the 15th was redeployed to Nagorno-Karabakh, to maintain the ceasefire that ended the third war between Armenia and Azerbaijan. The brigade consisted of three motorised rifle battalions, and one battalion each of tanks, anti-aircraft missiles, anti-aircraft missiles and artillery, and engineers, and was one of the first in the VSRF to include a company operating unmanned aerial vehicles (UAVs).

Russian Commanders
Nominal overall commander of the VSRF forces involved in the invasion of Chernihiv Oblast was Colonel General Alexandr Lapin, commander of the Operational Strategic Command Centre (OSK Centre). He graduated from the Kazan Higher Tank Command School in 1988, and in 2007 rose to the position of the CO 20th Guards Motor Rifle Division. After graduating from the Military Academy of the General Staff of the Armed Forces of the Russian Federation (GenStab), in 2017, he was appointed the chief-of-staff of the Russian Group of Forces in Syria. From October 2018 to January 2019, Lapin commanded this group, too. Back to Russia, in 2020, he graduated from the faculty of retraining and advanced training of the highest command personnel of the Military Academy of the GenStab.[12]

As of February 2022, the 41st CAA was commanded by Lieutenant General Sergey Borisovich Ryzhkov. He was born in Voronezh, in

Colonel General Alexander Lapin. (MoD Russian Federation)

1968, and is known to have graduated from the Leningrad Higher Combined Arms Command School in 1989. After serving in different motor rifle units – he graduated from the Mikhail Frunze Combined Arms Academy in 1999. Following participation in the First and Second Chechen Wars, he commanded the 39th Motor Rifle Brigade, before graduating from the GenStab Academy in 2015. Ryzhkov commanded the 29th Combined Arms Army from 2017 to 2019, then the 58th Combined Arms Army (where he served a tour of duty in Syria), before being reassigned to the 41st CAA, in August 2020.

The Chief-of-Staff of the 41st CAA was Major General Vitaly Petrovich Gerasimov (no relation to the chief of the GenStab in Moscow, Army General Valeriy Vasilyevich Gerasimov). He is known to have graduated from the Kazan Tank Higher Command School in 1999, then to have served in different roles in the North Caucasus, Far East, Southern, and Central military districts, advancing from the position of platoon commander to the chief-of-staff of a brigade. In 2014, he was involved in the initial Russian invasion of Ukraine while commanding the 15th Motor Rifle Brigade. Gerasimov subsequently served as head of the Tactics Department of the Russian Combined Arms Academy, from 2014 to 2017, before commanding the 90th Tank Division, from 2019 to 2020. He was appointed the Chief-of-Staff of the 41st CAA in 2020.

As of February 2022, the 2nd Guards Combined Arms Army was commanded by Major General Vyacheslav Nikolaevich Gurov. He is known to have served with motor rifle troops through the Second Chechen War, before commanding the 6th Tank Brigade, from 2010 to 2012. Over the following five years, Gurov commanded the 74th Guards Motor Rifle Brigade, and then, starting in 2017, the 90th Guards Tank Division. In 2019, Gurov was appointed the deputy commander of the 2nd GCAA, before being reappointed the Chief-of-Staff of the 58th CAA, in May 2021. By assumed the command of the 2nd GCAA in late 2021.

Following Gurov's death in combat, his successor became Lieutenant General Andrei Vladimirovich Kolotovkin. He is known to have entered military service after graduating from the Saint Petersburg Higher All-Arms Command School in 1990. In 1994, he commanded a motorised rifle platoon of the North Caucasian Military District, and subsequently progressed through command positions while participating in combat operations in Chechnya and Dagestan. From 2015 to 2016, Kolotovkin commanded the 8th Independent Guards Motor Rifle Brigade, and then served as the deputy commander of the Black Sea Fleet Coastal Troops in the Crimea. In 2018, he was appointed the Chief-of-Staff of the 8th Guards Combined Arms Army, and in 2020, the CO 2nd Guards Combined Arms Army.

Of the lower-ranking VSRF commanders, such are known as Colonel Barilo Denys Oleksandrovych (born in 1980) of the 15th Motor Rifle Brigade, and Colonel Yershov Pavlo Oleksiyovych (born in 1981) of the 74th Motor Rifle Brigade. However, due to the traditional style of command within the VSRF, their influence on the overall flow of the fighting remained extremely limited.

2
THE BATTLEFIELD

The Chernihiv region is one of the largest regions of Ukraine in terms of area (31,900 square kilometres, which is 5.3 percent of the territory of Ukraine), but sparsely populated: as of 1 January 2022, only about 959,300 thousand people lived on its territory. The region borders on the Russian Federation (225.09km of the state border), the Republic of Belarus (232.61km of the state border), Sumy, Poltava, and Kyiv regions.

The Chernihiv region has significant agricultural potential and was one of the most agriculturally developed in Ukraine. In the Polissya region, potatoes and flax were grown alongside cereals, while in the forest-steppe region, cereals and sugar beets were cultivated.

The regional centre, the city of Chernihiv, is located in the northern part of Ukraine, at the confluence of the Desna (a tributary of the Dnipro) and Stryzhen (a tributary of the Desna) rivers in the Prydniprovska lowland, in the natural zone of Ukrainian Polissia. The distance to Kyiv is 209km by rail and 141km by road. As of January 2022, the population was approximately 285,000 people.

The other two major urban centres of Chernihiv Oblast are Nizhyn and Pryluky. Nizhyn was a modern, administrative, political, socio-economic, historical, cultural and intellectual centre of Chernihiv Oblast located on the highway connecting Kyiv with Moscow and the highway connecting Kyiv with Kipti and Hlukhiv. Even more importantly – especially from the point of view of the GenStab in Moscow, because the VSRF was heavily dependent on railways for its supplies – Nizhyn was a major railway hub on the connection of two railway links: one from Kyiv to Moscow, and the other from Chernihiv to Poltava. As of 2020, the city was populated by 68,000 people.

Located in the south of Chernihiv Oblast, and on the banks of the Uday River, 135km from Kyiv, Pryluky was another important industrial town and railway junction. As of 2022, it was populated by 51,600 people.

As of early 2022, the geography of the Chernihiv region was characterised by a large number of extensive forests: these covered over 20 percent of the Oblast's territory. Another notable characteristic is its rivers: 1,570 rivers with a total length of about 8,500km flow through the region. During the Russian all-out invasion, these severely restricted the actions of both the Russians and the Ukrainian forces and, as a result, were the principal reason why the VSRF units proved unable to establish a working logistics system and then bypass Chernihiv in order to storm Kyiv.

Chernihiv

Chernihiv is one of the oldest cities of Eastern Europe. Founded in the late seventh century, it was first mentioned in chronicles in 907, when its residents took part in the victorious campaign of the Kyivan Prince Oleg to Constantinople, the capital of the Eastern Roman Empire. Oleg then negotiated a peace treaty, in which Chernihiv was mentioned as second most important city in Oleg's possessions, and an important political, commercial, cultural and religious centre.

In 1026, the huge Chernihiv principality emerged in the Southern Rus, stretching from the modern-day Moscow region in the north, to the Crimean Peninsula in the south. Notable local rulers of the time were Volodymyr Monomakh, 'the storm of the Polovtsian steppe', 'the hero of the Tale of Igor's Campaign'; Ihor Sviatoslavych; and Mykhailo Vsevolodovych (killed by Tatars and later sainted). Many of the Chernihiv princes later became Grand Dukes of Kyiv. During its heydays, in the twelfth and thirteenth centuries, Chernihiv was also one of the largest cities in Europe.

In the mid-fourteenth century, Chernihiv, along with other southern Russian lands, became part of the Grand Duchy of Lithuania, and in the early sixteenth century the entire Chernihiv-Siverskaya land became part of the Moscow state. In 1618, Chernihiv

Coat of Arms of Chernihiv

and the entire Siverskyi area became part of Poland, but not for long, 30 years later the city was liberated from the Polish gentry by the rebellious Cossacks. At the same time, the Chernihiv Cossack Regiment, a military and administrative unit of the newly created Cossack state, the Hetmanate, was founded. In 1654, after the Pereyaslav Rada, Chernihiv, like the entire Cossack autonomy, was annexed to the Russian state.

After the final liquidation of the Hetmanate and the regimental system of Ukraine, Chernihiv became the centre of the Chernihiv governorate in 1782, the Little Russia province in 1796, and the Chernihiv province in 1802.

In the twentieth century, Chernihiv shared the fate of many other Ukrainian cities: revolutions, wars, and famines.

Chernihiv in early twentieth century. (Author's collection)

3
OPENING MOVES

While no details about the Russian planning have been officially released – by Kyiv or Moscow – a lot can be deducted on the basis of the flow of VSRF operations. The plan secretly drafted by the President of the Russian Federation, Vladimir Putin, his Minister of Defence, Sergey Shoigu, and the Chief of the GenStab, Valery Gerasimov, closely resembled Soviet operations in Czechoslovakia in 1968, and Afghanistan in 1979. The essence of the idea was to rapidly secure several airports in the Kyiv area, reinforce the special operations and airborne troops involved, and then seize control over the civilian and military administration. Elsewhere, the VSRF was to march in, pass through and then isolate the capital with motorised infantry and tanks.

Correspondingly – and because this plan was shared with the commanders of the involved combined arms armies only about 48 hours before the invasion was about to start – whatever Ryzhkov and Gurov were able to prepare in terms of planning, was probably of little more than orientation purposes for their subordinates. Constantly pushed by Putin, who – reportedly – was micromanaging a lot of operations early during the invasion, principally through making telephone calls directly to field commanders – the idea was to secure key points in Chernihiv Oblast through simultaneous and rapid advance from the international border in southern and western directions. Chernihiv was to be seized by the 41st CAA on the first day. On the eastern flank, a large detachment from the 90th Tank Division was to cross the Desna River and continue in southern direction, so to drive into the back of Ukrainian defences of Nizhyn and Pryluky, where the Ukrainians were in control of potentially strong blocking positions. In turn, these manoeuvres were not only to open the way for the 41st CAA's advance on Kyiv from the north-east, but especially for the major blow: the rush by the 2nd GCAA, and the 1st Guards Tanks Army from the east, via Krolevets and Baturin to Nizhyn, and via Sumy, Romny, to Pryluky – and from there in the direction of the Ukrainian capital.

According to what is known about the Russian intelligence assessments, the population of Chernihiv was expected to welcome the invaders with open arms. Correspondingly, leading units were deployed in marching order and nobody expected them to have to storm any kind of densely built-up urban areas. In the case of any problems, lower-ranking commanders were advised to block off the towns and cities in question, report, and then wait for orders.

Russian military intelligence can be assessed to have obtained most details about the Ukrainian defence planning, but the ZSU was not expected to offer more than token resistance.

On the Ukrainian side, defence planning had been changed several times since 2014, depending on the latest developments on the geo-strategic plan, and resulting intelligence assessments. For example, as of 2019, the defence of the eastern side of Kyiv was to be provided by the 1st Tank Brigade. However, only holding operations were planned for Chernihiv, mainly by sabotaging local bridges. Instead, the 1st was to fall back to Brovary, an eastern suburb of the capital, and try stopping the Russians there. As the events of late February and early March 2022 were to show, this part of the plan was radically revised over the following two years.

Since the autumn of 2021, but especially in late January and early February 2022, during the command and staff exercise Zametil-2022, the Ukrainians were running regular exercises in reacting to a Russian invasion in the direction of Chernihiv. As a result, elements of the 1st Tank Brigade began deploying north and north-east of the city of Chernihiv. According to the CO of the brigade, Leonid Khoda, the exercise involved rehearsing the deployment of armoured groups into designated areas, securing selected firing lines, and repelling enemy attacks. Moreover, during some exercises, the brigade left some of its equipment hidden near selected positions, and had hidden some of its T-64s and BMP-1s inside Chernihiv, while removing all the fuel and ammunition from its warehouses in Honcharivske.[1]

Strike on the Border Guards
Nominally at least, the Russian invasion was to commence at 05.00hrs local time, on 24 February 2024. However, due to security-related issues, and also general chaos within the chain of command of the VSRF, numerous units started fighting and advancing much earlier. Indeed, the 41st CAA's spearheads commenced their advance into Chernihiv Oblast at 04.20hrs – even before Putin's televised speech about the start of the war: that was the point in time at which the outpost of the 105th Prince Volodymyr the Great Detachment of the Dniprovske Border Guard Service, south of Pustynky and west of Chernihiv, was hit. The commander of the Dniprovske Border Guard Service, Colonel Oleksandr Chornyi, recalled: 'On February 24, 2022, 04:32, I received a report about crossing the state border by an unknown UAV that dropped explosives on the border outpost located in "Dniprovske" and five servicemen were injured'.[2]

Dmytro Bryzhynskyi, then still assigned to the Operational Command North, similarly recalled: 'At 04.20hrs, an SMS came from the duty officer for the border detachment in Dniprovskoe, reporting that his position was overflown by UAVs. I thought that the provocations began, because UAVs were something weak….'[3]

Gauging by the content of whatever official reports were subsequently released, the conclusion is that the UAV actually guided the Russian artillery fire from the territory of the Republic of Belarus. The shell – probably 152mm calibre – wounded not just five, but seven Border Guards. The most seriously injured was Victor Derevyanko: a piece of shrapnel flew through his hand into his stomach and embedded itself near his heart. He recalled: 'We were woken up approximately at 04.15hrs. There were explosions. The guys were hit in beds and I couldn't get up to get my bearings: [I] was bleeding from [my] hand'.

Although shocked by the attack, the Border Guards accomplished their task and quickly blew up the Ukrainian side of the bridge on the P56 Highway at several points, making it completely useless for the enemy: the 41st CAA was thus prevented from advancing on Chernihiv from the west, along the shortest route.[4]

Missile Strikes
Further to the rear inside Ukraine, one of the first military facilities to find itself on the receiving end of missile strikes was the base of the 1st Tank Brigade in Honcharivske. There, the Russians mainly targeted the compound used for training of recently recalled reservists. The commander of the brigade, Colonel Khoda, recalled:

We expected that there would still be a blow. That was confirmed at 05:00. We prepared psychologically and morally. Of course, there was no idea that there would be a full-scale war. But they were ready. The commander of the operational command, General Nikoliuk, called late on 23 February. Alerted me. I first gathered my deputies. During the night, we discussed who goes where. And in fact, at 04:00, the whole brigade was near its vehicles and ready to go. At 05.00hrs in the morning, we drove out.

The last cars left Honcharivske. This is a medical company. And just after they left, 5 minutes later, a rocket arrived. When the rocket arrived at 05:00, the chief-of-staff and the deputies checked the readiness of the closed, buried command post. There was a powerful detonation there. We understood that the war had begun. Indeed, it was a little unclear, but there was no panic. Some of the girls were afraid, but there was no chaos. Everyone ran where needed, performed tasks. Fortunately, no one was hurt by this blow. After half an hour, the entire brigade had left Honcharivske.

Another point hit by the opening salvo of the Russian ballistic and cruise missiles was the civilian airfield outside Nizhyn, now a base of the State Emergency Service. There, a missile hit the command and control centre, killing five – a colonel of the police and four civilian employees.[5] One of the survivors, Oleg Volinets, head of the meteorological service, recalled:

I was then at the command and control post. On 23 February, I went on 24-hour duty from 9 to 9 in the morning. It was February, it was dark, and the probable hit by a Kalibr cruise missile occurred around 05.40 of 24 February. I expected that there would be a war, but I did not think that they would start dropping bombs on people. Rather, I was aware that they would hit the runway to disable it so that the planes could not take to the sky. And yes, they disabled the command and control centre in order to make it impossible or difficult for planes to take off and land.

According to unofficial reports from Belarus, the airfield was also targeted by 9K720 Iskander (ASCC/NATO reporting name 'SS-26 Stone') ballistic missiles of the 448th Missile Brigade of the VSRF from positions in the Mozyr area.[6]

A scene from Nizhyn airfield after a Russian missile strike on 24 February 2022. (Ministry of Emergency Situations of Ukraine)

NIZHYN AIRFIELD

Located four kilometres north of Nizhyn, the local airfield was originally constructed as a base for bombers of the Long-Range Aviation. Since around 1964, it mainly housed Tupolev Tu-22s of the 199th Independent Long-Range Reconnaissance Aviation Regiment, tasked with operations against targets in western Europe. Following the collapse of the USSR, the 199th was reorganised as the 18th Independent Long-Range Aviation Squadron of the Ukrainian Air Force.

On 22 February 1999, the Ukrainian Parliament transferred this unit to the Ministry of Emergencies, and the unit was redesignated the 300th Special Aviation Squadron. Six years later, in November 2005, it was reorganised again, as the Special Aviation Detachment of the Operational and Rescue Service of the Civil Protection of the Ministry of Emergency of Ukraine. As of February 2022, the 300th Squadron was operating two Antonov An-26s, two Antonov An-30s, five Airbus H.225 Super Puma helicopters, five Antonov An-32Ps, two Eurocopter EC.145s, and four Mil Mi-8s. All the transports were flown to Poland on 23 February, while helicopters were scattered at various sites around the country.

Tu-22M in service with the Ukrainian Air Force, 1990s. (Author's collection)

Ground Invasion

Along the border, the fighting began at exactly 05.00hrs of 24 February, with massive Russian artillery barrages targeting the border crossings and positions controlled by the Ukrainian Border Guards. The heaviest hit were the crossings of Skytok, Novi Yarilovychi, and Hremiach north of Chernihiv, all of which were targeted by multiple volleys from BM-21 Grad MLRS. The ground advance began at 07.00hrs, when the leading column of the 35th Motor Rifle Brigade (35th MRB) moved along the road from Senkivka in the direction of Polissya. Shortly after, the spearhead of the 74th Guards Motor Rifle Brigade (74th GMRB) crashed through the border crossing of Skytok, and then rushed headlong down the E95 Highway. Both units were tasked with securing Chernihiv the same day: the speed of their advance was of such importance that the commanders of leading battalion tactical groups were ordered to quickly drive through, or bypass any settlements underway, and leave all Ukrainian flags in their place. The situation was similar further in the east, where the spearhead of the 90th Tank Division moved via the border crossing north of Mykolaivka and quickly reached Semenivka before continuing in a southern direction. In turn, the 105th Border Guards Detachment was left with no other choice but to commence a rapid withdrawal, away from the border, along secondary roads in a southern direction. Underway, its elements took care to blow up as many bridges as they could, to slow down the enemy advance. Later in the afternoon, they joined the first elements of the ZSU as these began mining northern approaches to Chernihiv.

Still well to the south of the Russians, the first units of the ZSU moved into their positions later during the morning.

Inside the city of Chernihiv, the 119th Brigade of the Territorial Defence was mobilised (in a matter of a few hours, 3,500 reservists were drafted into the ZSU's garrison of the city) and, supported by the local population, began setting up checkpoints, engineering barriers, and firing positions around the western, northern, and eastern side of the city. Its elements deployed in Nizhyn and Pryluky were doing the same, and also guarding important buildings in both towns.

On the contrary, the situation of the 58th Motorised Brigade, ZSU was very serious right from the start of the Russian onslaught. Deployed in the northern Sumy Oblast, its commander, Colonel Kashchenko, had no option of advancing his troops to selected positions. Instead, he had to order a general withdrawal. Based in Shostka, its 13th Battalion – and the accompanied 2nd Shostka Battalion of the National Guard – was ordered to fall back to Baturyn, before the spearheads of the 2nd GCAA could reach the town. In Sumy, the 15th Battalion was forced to rapidly withdraw in the direction of Konotop: not only to help protect the brigade's headquarters, but also to avoid being encircled by massive columns of the VSRF, that were bypassing the city both to the north and south. The 16th Battalion fell back from Hlukhiv in the direction of Baturyn, but was hit by several advancing Russian columns and suffered losses.

Above: A BMP-1 of the 1st Tank Brigade during an exercise Zametil-2022, in January 2022. (Ukrainian MOD)

Left: Russian troops crossing the border at Senkivka, early on 24 February 2022. (Screenshot from security camera)

A 2S3 self-propelled howitzer of the 1st Tank Brigade, ZSU, seen on the road to Chernihiv, at 10.08hrs on 24 February 2022. (Author's collection)

Anti-tank barricades on the streets of Chernihiv, April 2022. (Author's collection)

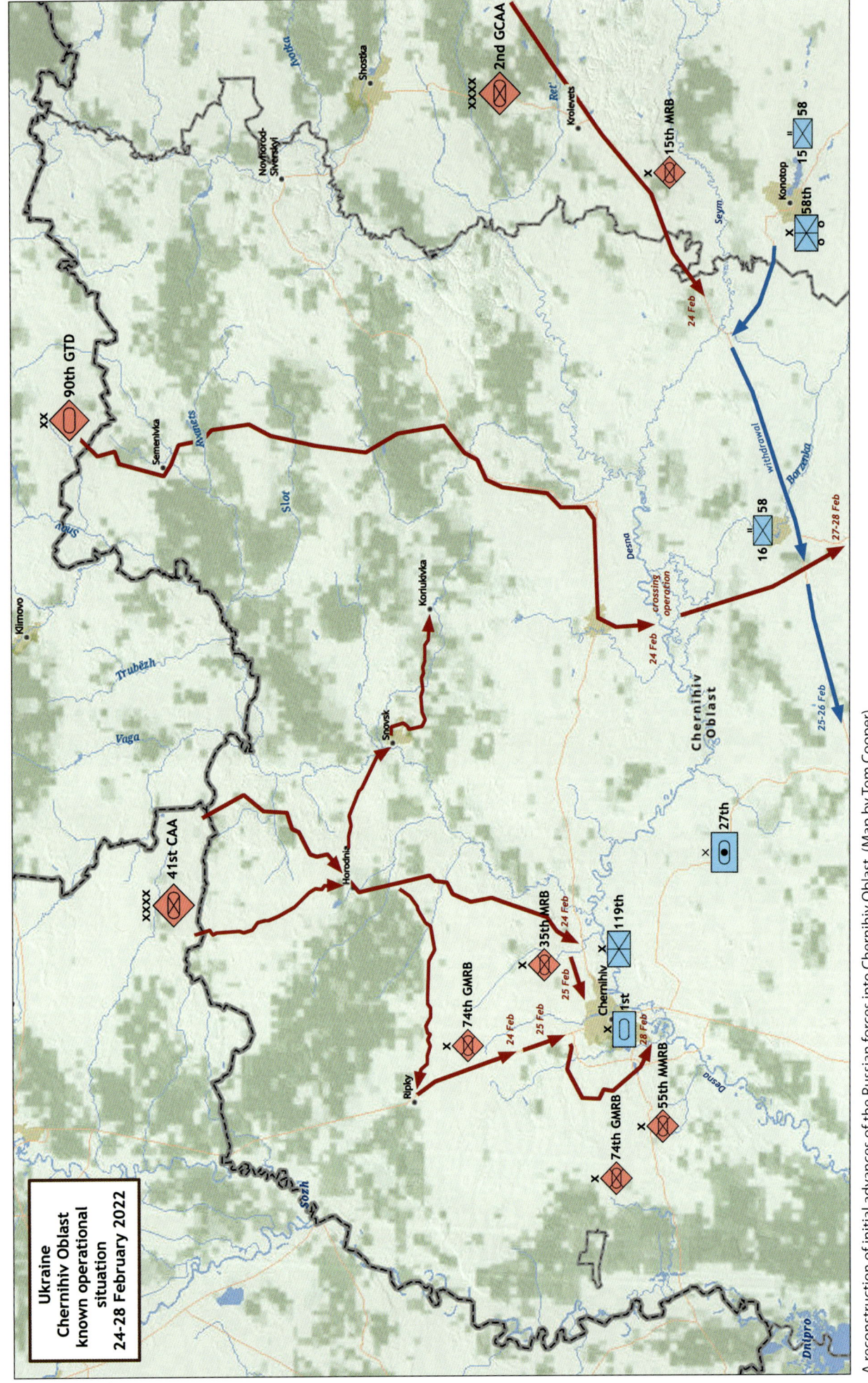

A reconstruction of initial advances of the Russian forces into Chernihiv Oblast. (Map by Tom Cooper)

4
ASSAULTS ON CHERNIHIV

The initial Russian advance on Chernihiv, Baturyn, Konotop and Sumy was extremely fast. Despite often very long distances they had to travel, by the afternoon of 24 February, long columns of VSRF armoured vehicles had reached points 35km north of Chernihiv. North of the city, a 34-kilometre-long Russian column had secured Semenivka, Horodnya, and Novhorod-Siverskyi. In the east, the VSRF columns had passed Krolevets and were on the approaches to Baturyn; had approached the eastern side of Konotop; and had bypassed Sumy on both its northern and southern side (the southern route was eventually cut off by the withdrawing 15th Battalion blowing up a highway bridge south of the city). That said, by that point in time, and except for a series of minor, running firefights with elements of the 16th Battalion of the ZSU, they did not encounter any major Ukrainian units.

Collision in Velyki Osniaky

The situation changed as the spearhead of the 74th GMRB approached Velyki Osniaky, a village about 25 kilometres north of Chernihiv. There, a company-strong detachment of the Mechanised Battalion from the 1st Tank Brigade, and a few T-64s of the 12th Independent Tank Battalion was in the process of travelling in a column up the E95 Highway, before turning east to head for the Koryukivka district. Because neither side knew about the enemy presence nearby, and did not expect a fight, a chaotic battle ensued, in which the Russians attacked head-on with their motorised infantry, while trying to flank the Ukrainians with tanks.

Commander of the Training Battalion of the Desna Training Centre, Major Artem Linkov, recalled:

> …we were in the village of Kiynka. The officer from Operational Command North arrived to announce, "A column is coming from the Gomel side, the battle has started and something is wrong with our guys, there is a sag in the defence!". They did not have time to move to the defence in time. And the situation, whether we are them, or they are us, was quite controversial. Two columns met, a counter-battle took place and it is not clear who is who.

As Linkov and his troops reached the scene of the fighting, they ran into two broken columns and several overturned and burning BMPs:

> I looked, there was an armoured personnel carrier standing and looking at me like that. I say to the gunner: "Do you see that armoured personnel carrier? Fire!" He is like: "What, really shoot at a BMP?". Yes, indeed, it is not a target! He fired a shot from this tank, the turret is blown away. I say to the driver-mechanic, go to the side, let's go to the side. Then we are waiting for what happens next. We got there, there was a dead Russian soldier lying next to the KAMAZ truck. Then they started looking at the equipment. I approach everyone and say the same phrase: "Are there killed, wounded, alive?". If there are, then surrender, if not, then I throw a grenade. Silence, fine. I open the landing hatches, there is no one. There was one Tiger, still operational: the guys from the infantry took it away.

By the time both sides withdrew, two Russian BMP-2s, two KAMAZ armoured trucks, and several Tigr-M infantry mobility vehicles were destroyed, and 30 VSRF troops killed or wounded. One Russian – Sergeant Konstantin Buynichev – was captured, together with one of the Tigr-Ms. In turn, the 1st Tank lost two BMP-1s and six troops killed.

The next clash followed shortly after in the Ripky area – well-known to the troops of the 1st Tank Brigade, because they had exercised there only a week before. It developed when a mechanised company of this brigade was sent to stall the further advance of the 74th GMRB down the E95. Khoda recalled:

> Their reinforced company tactical group was driving with tanks, at full speed. So we pulled the tanks away and ambushed them. I still had time to call the battalion commander, the communications were working. I told him to let them approach and order the artillery to work. And we started with the battery, and so their first column was almost completely destroyed at the front. They did not even understand anything. They thought it was their artillery covering them, I guess.
>
> Their second column followed the same path. We took a captive and asked that fool: "Why did you even go there?" And he said: "We were told those were destroyed Ukrops' tanks".

As this engagement was developing, Linkov's reserve element of three tanks was rushed forward. Much to the Lieutenant Colonel's displeasure, his own T-64BV broke down, while the second one began overheating – probably due to degraded maintenance, caused by operating from dispersed positions for three weeks. This left him with only one T-64, and two BMPs. Nevertheless, elements of the 119th Brigade were present, as recalled by Junior Lieutenant Kostyantyn Derevyanko, who served with the 1st Rifle Company:

> …we received information that enemy tanks were moving towards Chernihiv, and we had to stop them. An officer lined us up, issued RPG-22, RPG-26 grenade launchers to those who know how to work with them. They set the task of taking positions near the road and shooting at the first and last tank so that the column stopped. At the same time, one of our comrades, Konstantin, was assigned the task of creating an additional obstacle for the tanks on the road, after the third shot of the tanks, he had to drive the KAMAZ onto the road and block it. He also performed this very risky task, even though he was a direct target for enemy tanks.

A group of operators of rocket-propelled grenades (RPGs), including Derevyanko, then quickly changed positions before additional enemy vehicles arrived. Dereveyanko hit the first tank, causing it to stop and start emitting smoke:

> When a tank drove down the road right in front of me, I decided to shoot at its undercarriage, as my comrades advised me. After all, with an RPG, you can't do much trouble to such a vehicle, but: it is quite possible to immobilise it. Yes, actually,

it turned out. With the first shot, I hit the tank in the front part of the track. It violently turned around, coming to a halt on the side of the road. Immediately after me, while the tank was still moving, my brother Anatoliy fired a shot in the area of the tank's turret.

The Russian T-72B was then hit by a Ukrainian T-64 and set afire, thus buying time for the Ukrainian RPG operators to redeploy again. One of the soldiers was then sent in a northern direction, to scout:

> Because two of our men did not withdraw to the new position, one comrade, Serhiy, was given a grenade launcher and sent to see what happened to them. When he left, there was an automatic queue. I look – Sergey is walking, and in front of him is a man with a headset. This was our first prisoner. He was brought to our position and we asked who he was, what was his rank and position. Then he told us that he was a gunner-operator, but it turned out that he was a tank commander. We've learned about this only later, from a YouTube-interview with Volodymyr Zolkin. Our boys were ready to tear that Russian apart, but the senior officer and I did not allow him to be touched. We searched his uniform but he had nothing on him: no documents, no phone, no other things. He said that everything was taken before they advanced to Chernihiv Oblast. He also reported that there were three tanks and two infantry fighting vehicles, he was from the first tank. We asked how many there are. He replied that the tank battalion was coming, and these were 28–30 tanks. He also said that there was another Russian soldier wounded in the leg, laying on the ground from where he came. But, the commander did not allow us to go back for him, because it was risky and we did not know for sure whether he was still alive or not. After a while, when we did patrol that spot, he was gone. Later, it turned out that he climbed out onto the road and was picked up by local residents of the dachas, who provided assistance. And he lived there until April 3. After the liberation of Chernihiv Oblast, he was handed over to the police.
>
> There was also a third – a gunner. He was seriously injured and eventually died. At first his body was left where found, in the forest. But I decided that we should bury him. Together with his brothers, on April 13, we dug a hole and buried him so that he would not lie in the forest. By the way, this was also a controversial moment, because some guys were categorically against such an act. But I have another opinion. We are not Russians, and in any situation, we must remain human. And it was humane to bury him, which, in fact, we did.[1]

As a consequence of this shocking loss, not only was the spearhead of the 74th GMRB destroyed well before reaching Chernihiv, but an entire Russian reconnaissance platoon surrendered. The initial advance of the 41st CAA thus came to a sudden, and very rude halt.

90th Tank Division reaches the Desna

Further east, the 90th Tank Division was making probably the best advance deep into northern Ukraine of all the VSRF units on that day. After passing Semenivka, the leading BTGs of the 80th Tank Regiment and the 228th Motor Rifle Regiment drove another 106 kilometres to reach the Makoshyne area, on the northern bank of the Desna River. Once there, they stopped while waiting for engineers to construct a pontoon bridge: their task was to cross the river, then reach the E101 Highway, turn west and cut off the E95 Highway south of Chernihiv, thus isolating this city from Kyiv.

Unexpectedly for the Russians – but to the good fortune of the Ukrainians – it was precisely at that point that the majority of the 16th Battalion, 58th Motorised Brigade, ZSU, reached the Velyka

A Russian T-72B Obr. 1989, from the 74th GMRB, seen after being knocked out outside Khalyavyn. (Author's collection)

View of the battle on Velyki Osniaky on 24 February 2022, from the side of the soldiers of the Mechanised Battalion, 1st Tank Brigade. (Author's collection)

Doch area, about 10 kilometres south of Makoshyne. As described above, the unit was on withdrawal from Hlukhiv. With help of local civilians, its scouts then found the Russian bridging operation and called down artillery fire on the pontoons. The Ukrainian 27th Rocket Artillery Brigade opened devastating fire, completely ruining the Russian crossing attempt, destroying at least one bridge and nine or 10 vehicles with the opening salvo from BM-27 multiple rocket launchers alone. According to Major General Nikolyuk, the 27th – repeatedly supported by the 19th Missile Brigade, which deployed a number of OTR-21 Tochkas – destroyed or damaged up to 60 Russian vehicles during subsequent Russian attempts to cross the Desna at Makoshyne, over the following two days.

The success of the ZSU's artillerists and missileers not only forced the 90th Tank Division to abandon the original plan to reach the M01 Highway south of Chernihiv: it also bought the time for not only the 16th Battalion, but the mass of the 58th Motorised Brigade to withdrew towards Nizhyn, where two of its battalions entrenched around the town, and one inside of it. Moreover, the 2nd Regiment National Guard managed to withdraw from the north-east and entrench in the Kozelets area.² Finally, the sappers of the 250th Engineering Support Centre were able to reach the Nizhyn area in time: the commander of that unit, Colonel Serhiy Burkovsky, then deployed his troops to block both the M02 and H07 highways. Although Burkovsky was wounded in one of the resulting clashes, his unit effectively stopped further advances of the 90th Tank Division and the entire 2nd GCAA in the Nizhyn area.³

All of this had far-reaching consequences for the coming battle, both for the northern Ukrainian stronghold and for Kyiv: not only that its garrison's communications to the capital remained open, but the 90th Tank Division also experienced massive delays even while trying to join the advancing elements of the 2nd GCAA in the Plysky area. In turn, the Russians failed to secure Nizhyn, then took until 1 March to find a suitable place to penetrate the Ukrainian defence line between that town and Pryluky, and until 9 March to reach Brovary – where their advance on the eastern side of the Ukrainian capital was ultimately stopped.

Ryzhkov's Second Attempt

During the evening of 24 February 2022, General Ryzhkov ordered the second BTG of the 74th GMRB into a probing attack on the village of Mykhailo-Kotsiubynske. The unit advanced down the section of the E95 Highway bypassing Chernihiv to the west, but ran into an ambush and was forced to withdraw. Although the Russians thus ended the day well outside the city, early the next morning the General Staff in Moscow boasted that Chernihiv was surrounded and there was 'lack of Ukrainian resistance'. Meanwhile, Ryzhkov was already organising the 74th's next attack: on the villages of on Polubotky and Khalyavyn, northern outskirts of Chernihiv.

Ambush of the 74th GMRB

After failing to reinitiate his advance into Chernihiv, General Ryzhkov was forced to regroup his forward units. In the process, he was experiencing ever growing problems: most of his manoeuvring was reported by local civilians to the ZSU, and an engineering column was hit by multiple Tochkas of the 19th Missile Brigade while parked in the village of Horodnya, on the P13 Highway and 19 Russian vehicles were completely destroyed. Another Russian column was ambushed further north and lost several vehicles and killed troops: the ZSU soldiers even managed to capture lots of documentation with personal data about enemy officers and other ranks.

Nevertheless, probably under growing pressure from Putin, Ryzhkov continued pushing. Next, he sent the second BTG of the 74th GMRB to attack down the E95 Highway. After passing Rivnopillya, this turned left to reach Khalyavyn, 13km from

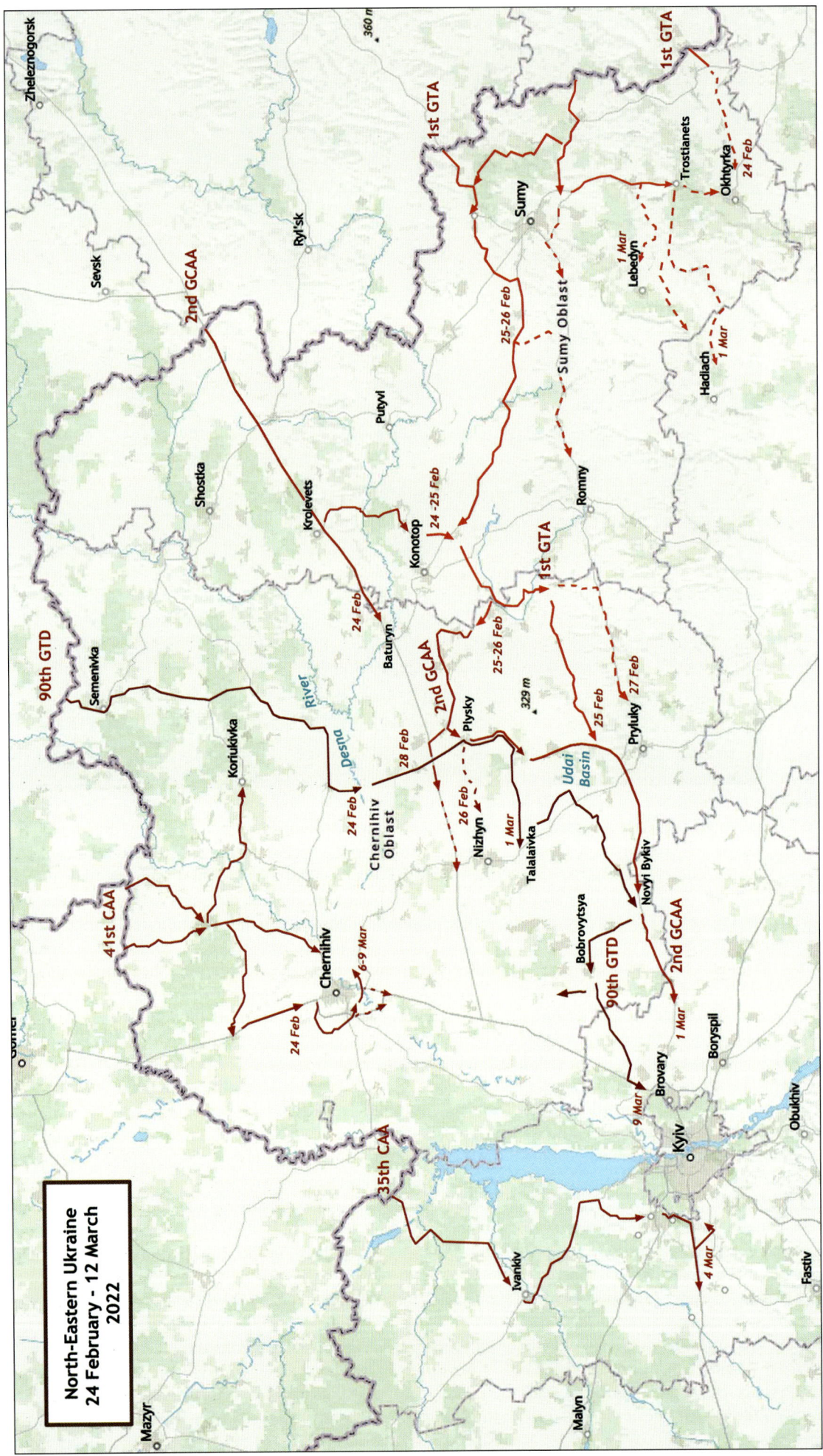

A map reconstructing advances of the VSRF into north-eastern Ukraine, 24 February – 12 March 2022. Notable is how the 2nd GCAA sought to bypass all the larger urban centres where its forces encountered Ukrainian resistance: first at Baturyn and Konotop, then in the Nizhyn area. The eastern part of the 90th Territorial Defence adopted this approach, followed by the 41st CAA, which eventually tried to bypass Chernihiv in order to reach the M01 Highway leading to Kyiv. (Map by Tom Cooper)

Destroyed T-64BV tank of the 1st Tank Brigade, seen after the battle in Khalyavyn on 25 February 2022. (Author's collection)

Chernihiv, but there ran into a checkpoint of the 1st Tank Brigade, manned by a mechanised infantry platoon with three BMP-1s, covered by two T-64BVs. According to the Ukrainian company commander Dmytro Ordynskyi, the approaching enemy column included about 50 vehicles: 'Everything went just as we had planned. We stopped them, the battle started, they deployed in combat formation, and our artillery began to fire, while we had to retreat to Chernihiv'.

In a direct tank battle, the Ukrainians knocked out two T-72s while losing one T-64 and having the turret of one of their BMP-1s pierced by a shell that failed to detonate. When the Russians then attempted to flank them on both sides, they were hit by an artillery barrage. This not only knocked out 10–15 Russian vehicles, but enabled Ordynskyi's company to withdraw in good order. Its damaged BMP was hit by two additional rounds, but still managed to limp back to the lines of the 22nd Battalion of the 27th National Guard Brigade in Polubotky. The advance of the 74th GMRB was thus stopped once again.

Failures of the 35th MRB
Repeated ambushes not only sapped the strength of the 41st CAA, but bought plenty of valuable time for the Ukrainian garrison of Chernihiv. By the end of 25 February, elements of the 1st Tank Brigade and the 119th Brigade TO were deployed around the city, while inside, other units and local residents were preparing to fight the Russians in urban warfare. Their preparations were still in full swing when, early on 26 February, Ryzhkov launched his next attempt to reach the city.

At 6.00 in the morning, two successive columns of the leading BTG of the 35th MRB approached north-eastern Chernihiv. The first rolled down the P13 Highway before turning west to continue along the P12, and then losing their way: by accident, it passed a checkpoint of the National Guard unmolested, before wandering deep into the north-eastern part of the city. Around 06.30hrs, it almost reached the Epicenter supermarket, when it was ambushed by a company of about 70 troops from the 22nd Battalion and volunteers of the 119th Brigade, supported by four T-64 tanks. In the ensuing chaos, the Russians lost two T-72s, a BMP-2, and a BTR-80 wheeled armoured personnel carrier with the 35th MRB's chief of communications, Lieutenant Colonel Nikolai Pirozhkov.

Consisting of seven T-72s and seven BMP-2s, the second column approached Pivtsi airfield around 10.30hrs. Fortunately for Ukraine, the latter was now well protected: an infantry company from the 22nd Battalion National Guard was entrenched there, together with five T-64s of the 1st Tank Brigade. Sergeant-Major Volodymyr Kyslovets recalled:

They first attempted to break through to the airfield, but our tankers hit four of their tanks. When a tank is not burning, it is smoking white, so our tankers were shooting these clouds of smoke. They did a great job and never missed the target. They remained in cover and were almost invisible. Whenever the enemy appeared, they moved forward, shoot, and then retreated.

Indeed, the first Russian T-72B was hit while still about one kilometre east of the airport. It was commanded by Major Leonid Shchetkin, battalion commander in the 35th MRB. A hit to the track caused it to go out of control: the second and then the third hit killed the driver, Dmytro Opoikov, and set the vehicle afire, forcing Shchetkin and his gunner, Staff Sergeant Mykhailo Kulikov to bail out and hide inside a nearby barn where they were captured shortly after. Another T-72B was disabled by the infantry of the Territorial Defence, which also claimed a BMP-2 as destroyed. With their commander captured, the Russians then retreated in disarray, abandoning one T-72B, one BMP-1, and a R-166-0.5 mobile radio station, which the Ukrainians captured intact.[4] The subsequent interrogation of the Russian prisoners of war revealed that Shchetkin's group was supposed to 'merely' screen off the city, but lost direction.

Indeed, the capture of Shchetkin and the death of Pirozhkov were severe blows for the 35th MRB. Not only had the latter played a crucial role in maintaining the communications network of the brigade, but the former was the only officer fully informed about the mission: his subordinates had little understanding of the situation and were not trained to act on their own. Unsurprisingly, the 35th withdrew in disorder, and the 41st CAA never attempted another direct assault into Chernihiv again.[5]

On 27 February 2022, General Ryzhkov launched his final attempt to enter Chernihiv, this time from the village of Novyi Bilous, north-west of the city. This was a large-scale assault by BTGs from the 74th

Russian T-72B Obr. 1989 from the 35th Motor Rifle Brigade seen in Chernihiv on 26 February 2022. The vehicle wreck has become a popular place for taking photographs, both by residents and visiting journalists. (Author's collection)

GMRB and the 55th Mountain Motor Rifle Brigade (55th MMRB), that pressed the Ukrainians hard before it was repelled. The success came at a price. Amongst others, the 1st Tank Brigade lost a T-64BV hit by two anti-tank missiles (probably 9M133 Kornet; ASCC/NATO reporting name 'AT-14 Spriggan'). The vehicle went up in flames, killing its entire crew, including Senior Lieutenant Maksym Bilokon, driver Junior Sergeant Dmytro Kaplin, and the gunner, Ivan Koval. Also killed was another tankman of this brigade: Chief Sergeant Oleksiy Senyuk fell to an artillery barrage that hit the area near the Epicenter supermarket. He was posthumously awarded the title Hero of Ukraine and the Order of the Golden Star for courage.[6]

Inside the city, the Russians – almost certainly on the basis of intelligence provided by a local informants – targeted the area of the ZSU stronghold near the Epicenter supermarket with an Iskander-M missile. This killed at least one tank crewman of the 1st Tank Brigade, and was immediately followed by severe artillery barrage that, amongst others, destroyed another T-64.

Two soldiers of the 119th Brigade Territorial Defence in the first days of the Russian invasion. (Author's collection)

5
THE BYPASS ATTEMPT

With all attempts of Ryzhkov's 41st CAA to enter Chernihiv failing, on 28 February 2022, the Russians gave up the idea of assaulting the city. Instead, they returned to the original plan to bypass Chernihiv and resume their advance in the direction of Kyiv. Thus began the second phase of the battle.

The Clover-Sparta Position
Early on 28 February, a BTG of the 55th MMRB attacked down the E95 Highway bypassing Chernihiv to the west. Initially, all the resulting assaults failed, because a weak company of Ukrainian infantry, supported by two T-64 MBTs, made excellent use of the terrain between Lhiv, Staryi Bilous, Zaitsi and Kyinka, the four western suburbs of the city.

Nominally, the strongest ZSU position in this area was nicknamed 'Sparta' because of harsh local conditions during the winter. It was situated within a forest surrounding a four-leaf-clover-shaped intersection of the E95 Highway, and the P56 Highway, leading to the west. There, the Ukrainian infantry armed with assault rifles and only four RPGs fended off five half-hearted Russian assaults.

It was during the fighting in this area that, on 28 February, Ryzhkov's deputy, Major General Andrey Sukhovetsky, was shot dead by a Ukrainian sniper while trying to push the 55th MMRB forward. Eventually, while pinning down the Sparta position with massive barrages from BM-21 multiple rocket launchers, the second BTG of the 55th MMRB, followed by a BTG of the 74th GMRB – about 258 vehicles in total – advanced well to the west and, around 08.00hrs, managed to secure the village of Mykhailo-Kotsyubynske. This big concentration of armoured vehicles was promptly reported by the locals to the ZSU, and Mykhailo-Kotsyubynske was severely shelled by the 27th Artillery Brigade, which destroyed a number of logistic vehicles. Nevertheless, the Russians continued pushing and around 11.00hrs their spearheads reached Shestovystya on the northern bank of the Desna River. While the mobile command post of the 41st CAA was established at the Lan farm, in the western outskirts of the village, engineers of the 40th Engineer-Sapper Regiment were rushed forward to start constructing a pontoon bridge.

Bridgehead at Shestovystya
Despite constant reporting by local civilians, the Russian advance via Mykhailo-Kotsyubynske to Shestovystya took the Operational Command North completely by surprise. Indeed, not only were the Russian engineers able to construct their first pontoon bridge entirely unmolested by Ukrainian artillery, but Ryzhkov promptly rushed the 55th MMRB to the southern bank of the Desna River. It was only later during 28 February that a direct hit by a Tochka missile ripped the bridge apart, leaving its remaining sections to be swept downstream.

By this time the 41st CAA was in such a state of chaos that it took Ryzhkov three days to bring forward another bridge column and launch a new crossing attempt. The new bridge was in place on 28 February but was promptly subjected to murderous Ukrainian artillery fire and four Tochka strikes. Although hit several times, because its construction was originally meant for the Strategic Missile Forces its sections were foam-impregnated, this meant that even if badly damaged they did not sink. Such a bridge was what enabled the 55th MMRB to bring its second BTG over the river. This was followed by the second BTG of the 74th GMRB. Together, the two units expanded the bridgehead on the southern bank of the Desna through securing the villages of Ladynka, Zolontynka, and Yahidne. The 41st CAA was thus, finally, on the brink of achieving

A T-72B3 that was dropped into the Desna when a Ukrainian Tochka ballistic missile destroyed the Russian pontoon bridge outside Shestovystya on 28 February 2022. It is seen here while in the process of being recovered by Ukrainian engineers, in summer of the same year. (State Special Transport Service of Ukraine)

a breakthrough at the operational level, and pushing down the M01 Highway in the direction of Kyiv.

Major General Nikolyuk in person brought the 15th Battalion of the 58th Motorised Brigade from the east, along the P67 Highway. As he drove into Yahidne, his column ran into an ambush. Nikoyluk's driver was shot dead and several aides wounded. The General returned fire using an AK-74, RPG-22 and RPG-26s, until the 2A72 30mm autocannons of the Russian BTR-82s forced them to retreat. The efforts by the enterprising General to establish a defensive position at the junction of the E95 and M01 highways were spoiled by massive volumes of the Russian artillery fire. Nevertheless, early the next morning, Nikolyuk led a local counterattack to recover the body of his driver, and he and his aides destroyed a Tigr-M in the process.

Kolychivka
After repairing the damaged pontoon bridge at Shestovystya, on 5 March 2022 Ryzhkov deployed a BTG of the 90th Tank Division into a new attack, this time from Yahidne on Ivanivka, as recalled by General Nikolyuk: 'They covered Ivanivka with artillery, and they came in from several sides. The 58th Brigade was fighting. Unfortunately, all our armoured personnel carriers were destroyed. The enemy's equipment was destroyed, but about two companies came in, while we had only five BMPs and about 50 personnel there'.[1]

Gradually, the Russians knocked out all the Ukrainian IFVs and broke into the village, forcing the surviving ZSU troops to fall back. At this crucial moment, instead of using momentum to continue pushing, the 41st CAA stopped. The fact was that its units have entered Ukraine expecting little resistance. Correspondingly, they were carrying with them food, ammunition, and other supplies for only three days: the mass of which was spent or destroyed during early attacks on Chernihiv. Unsurprisingly, by 28 February, all the units were in urgent need of resupply. However, their logistic tail began falling apart: not only had the Ukrainians removed all road signs – to the point where even some ZSU units got lost, time and again – but they began deploying raiding parties behind the Russian rear, to ambush convoys moving in the southern direction. Combined with heavy losses in the chain of command, and total chaos in the communication system of the 41st CAA, their work completely ruined Ryzhkov's planning. Unsurprisingly, the General took two days to reorganise his mauled command to the level where this was capable of resuming the advance.

On 7 March 2022, Ryzhkov ordered the 90th Tank Division to complete the encirclement of Chernihiv through attacking north from Yahidne into the village of Kolychivka. This was held by two companies of the 15th Battalion, reinforced by elements of the 21st Independent Rifle Battalion, a company of the 2nd Regiment National Guard (which withdrew from Shostka), supported by two T-64BV tanks of the 58th Motorised Brigade. The garrison was commanded by Lieutenant Colonel Maksym Khrebtov.

Kolychivka had been intermittently shelled for two days before, early that morning, a column of four T-72s, four BMP-2s, and two MT-LB armoured personnel carriers, followed by several other vehicles, attacked. Taking the Ukrainians by surprise, the Russians breached the checkpoint at the southern entrance, thundered through the entire settlement up the main road, and encountered resistance only while reaching the northern side. There, they were hit by NLAWs and RPGs from several sides and lost a number of vehicles. The Ukrainian T-64BVs then hit two of the BMP-2s: when the infantry attempted to leave through their rear doors, they were cut down by the fire from assault rifles and machine guns. A soldier of the National Guard recalled: 'All of them remained in one of the BMPs, and we later saw their bodies. Our tankmen worked well on them. The Russians saw what would happen to them, and that's why

Kolychivka, seen after the fighting in summer 2022. (Author's collection)

Generally, the mass of VSRF motorised infantry units were equipped either with BMP-2s or BTR-82s. However, the 35th Motor Rifle Brigade – as well as the 57th and 60th Motor Rifle Brigades, the 5th Tank Brigade, and the 394th Motor Rifle Regiment of the 127th Motor Rifle Division – operated a total of about 300–350 ancient BMP-1s. This example from the 35th was captured on 26 February 2022. As of 2022, the Russians also operated a few BRM-1KG reconnaissance vehicles in their reconnaissance battalions. (Artwork by David Bocquelet)

The primary infantry combat vehicle of the motor rifle formations of the VSRF was the BMP-2. Introduced to service in the 1980s, this was an evolution of the BMP-1 design, mainly recognisable by a larger turret mounting the 2A42 30mm autocannon. The 14,300kg vehicle had a crew of three, and could carry up to seven fully armed infantrymen. Nominally, the BMP-2s could launch 9M113 Konkurs ATGMs, too, but these were rarely seen in service during the fighting in Chernihiv Oblast. This example was probably operated by the 74th GMRB. (Artwork by David Bocquelet)

The BTR-82A wheeled armoured carrier was a deeply modernised variant of the well-known BTR-82. Officially entering service in 2013, it had more powerful engine and improved manoeuvrability, improved armour and spall liners, a GLONASS navigation system, and mounted the 2A72 30mm autocannon in its turret. Since 2019, all vehicles of this type also received a new fire control system with thermal imager. This is a reconstruction of one of two BTR-82As was destroyed during the fighting for Kolychivka in early March 2022, which makes it likely that it was operated by the 90th Tank Division. (Artwork by David Bocquelet)

The T-72B Obr. 1989 (colloquially known as 'T-72BM', which is an unofficial, and incorrect designation) was a heavily modernised variant of the T-72B, including Kontakt-5 explosive reactive armour, and composite armour on the sides of the turret. This was a vehicle of the 35th Motor Rifle Brigade that was captured by Ukrainian troops north-east of Chernihiv. Painted in olive green overall, it received a crudely applied, diagonal white stripe down the side skirts, and a 'cope cage' supposed to protect it from top-attack weapons, like NLAW and Javelin ATGMs. (Artwork by David Bocquelet)

This T-72B was destroyed in Velyka Doroha, a village roughly half-way between Nizhyn and Pryluky, where Ukrainian artillery knocked out about 40 armoured vehicles of the 90th Tank Division and the 2nd Guards Combined Arms Army (nearly all were subsequently captured by the ZSU, repaired and pressed into service again). As frequently the case in February–March 2022, the vehicle was only partially equipped with Kontakt-1 explosive reactive armour, and painted in olive green overall. The insignia 'H2200' was a code for the Russian railway transport, indicating the tank was classified as 'oversized cargo'. (Artwork by David Bocquelet)

The T-72A was an earlier version of this prolific family, accepted into service with the Soviet Army in 1979. Being cheaper to manufacture than either T-72B or T-80B, it was manufactured in huge numbers, and thus thousands were still in service with the VSRF as of 2022. This example – equipped with KMT mine plough, and partially overpainted in white – was operated by the 239th Guards Tank Regiment of the 90th Guards Tank Division, until captured in Kolychivka, on 7 March 2022. (Artwork by David Bocquelet)

The primary medium-range air defence system of the VSRF as of February 2022 was the 9M317ME Buk-M3. A typical battery included four transporter-erector-launchers and radars (TELARs) as shown here (each capable of carrying eight surface-to-air missiles), and almost all the BTGs of the 41st CAA were protected by them. Due to the lack of Ukrainian opposition, though, the majority were held well to the rear. (Artwork by David Bocquelet)

Rather surprisingly for most of the VSRF, due to unexpectedly fierce Ukrainian resistance, and frequent ambushes of supply convoys, fuel trucks like this ATMZ-5-4320 (based on the chassis of the Ural-4320 truck) proved extremely important. Nominally, a column of some 12 was the centrepiece of every battalion supply platoon, regimental supply platoon and fuel supply company of every division. Dozens were captured by Ukrainian forces – and also by civilians – during the fighting in Chernihiv Oblast. (Artwork by David Bocquelet)

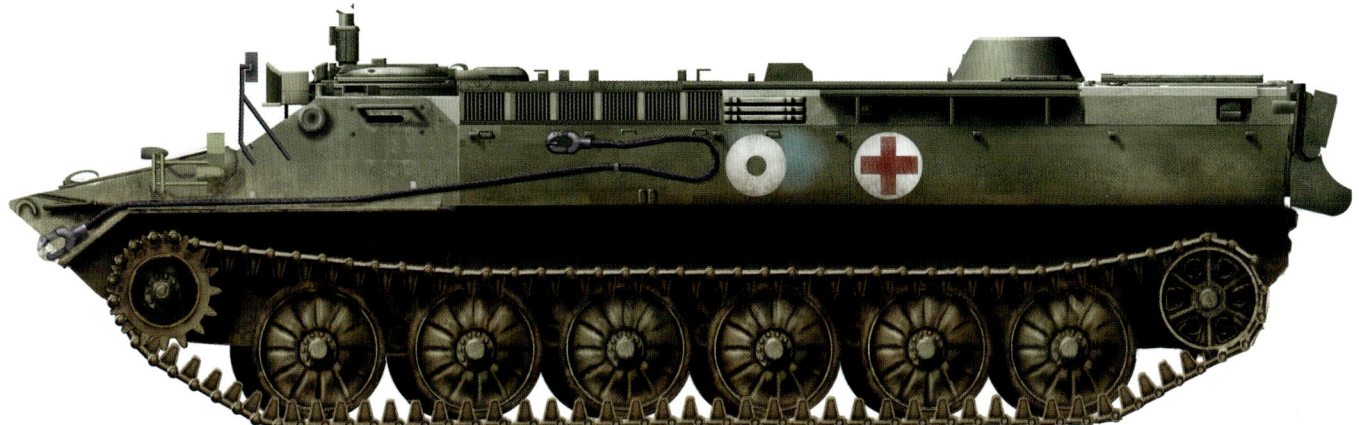

The MT-LB family of tracked armoured vehicles was designed to serve both as armoured personnel carriers and artillery tractors. This one was modified to serve as a battlefield ambulance and received attachments at the rear to support stretchers carrying the wounded. The vehicle was destroyed during the fighting for Lukashivka in early March 2022. (Artwork by David Bocquelet)

The ZSU lacked more modern BMP-2s, and thus the majority of its mechanised units went into the war still equipped with old BMP-1s. This example – which retained its old three-colour camouflage pattern left from Soviet times and was suitably nicknamed 'Chernigov' – was assigned to the 1st Tank Brigade. (Artwork by David Bocquelet)

The Anti-Aircraft Defence Battalion of the 1st Tank Brigade, ZSU, included a single battery equipped with 2K22 Tunguska self-propelled anti-aircraft defence systems, at least two of which are known to have been deployed inside Chernihiv during the siege. Each of the 35,000kg vehicles mounted eight-tube launchers for 9M311 surface-to-air missiles (range 8–10km), and two 2A38M 30mm autocannons, for which 1,904 rounds were carried. Ukrainian Tunguskas seem to have been left in olive green overall, and have worn no, or next to no markings except for the white cross on this example, which was heavily camouflaged by foliage, too. (Artwork by David Bocquelet)

The Anti-Aircraft Defence Battalion of the 1st Tank Brigade also operated a battery of older 9K35 Strela-10 tracked anti-aircraft systems. Each battery included four 9K35 TELARs, each armed with four 9M31M, 9M37, 9M37M, or 9M333 electro-optically and/or infrared guided surface-to-air missiles, with a range of 10km. Gauging by its digital camouflage pattern, this was one of the vehicles that underwent a major repair or overhaul since 2016. (Artwork by David Bocquelet)

WAR IN UKRAINE VOLUME 11: THE BATTLE OF CHERNIHIV, FEBRUARY–MARCH 2022

This was one of the T-64BVs of the 1st Tank Brigade seen during the defence of Chernihiv. This variant represented the backbone of the ZSU's tank fleet since 1992. Overhauled since 2016, it received the digital (or 'pixel') camouflage pattern atop of its olive green livery, while the yellow paint applied around the fume evacuator of the gun barrel identified it as belonging to the 1st Tank Brigade: its tanks have worn this insignia since taking part in the fighting in the Donbass in 2014–2015. (Artwork by David Bocquelet)

As of February–March 2022, the venerable 2S1 Gvozdika self-propelled 122mm howitzer was the primary artillery piece of all mechanised formations of the ZSU. The Artillery Group of the 1st Tank Brigade, for example, included a single 'divizion' equipped with 18 such equipments. All were painted in olive green overall, with a digital/pixel camouflage pattern in yellow sand, brick red, and black, but wore no insignia whatsoever. (Artwork by David Bocquelet)

As of 2014, the Ukrainian Army had withdrawn all of its 2S3 Akatsiya self-propelled 152mm howitzers from service. Although a number were subsequently overhauled, they remained a rare sight even as of 2022. However, the Artillery Group of the 1st Tank Brigade retained 18 Akatsiyas, and they were operational during the Battle of Chernihiv as well. As in the case of 2S1s, they were painted in olive green overall, with a digital/pixel camouflage pattern in yellow sand, brick red, and black. (Artwork by David Bocquelet)

Above left: This Russian infantryman of the 35th Motorised Rifle Brigade is shown wearing the typical 'Ratnik' uniform with Flora camouflage pattern. Atop of this, he donned a ballistic helmet and the Pantsyr cargo vest and plate carrier, but the latter were rarely issued. His firearm is an AK-105 assault rifle. The red bands around his arms and legs were the typical 'means of quick visual identification' for the troops of the 41st CAA during the Battle of Chernihiv. (Artwork by Giorgio Albertini)

Above right: During the Battle of Chernihiv, some of the Ukrainian units defending the city – or deployed south of it – were supplied with a small number of FGM-148 Javelin ATGMs, one of which is shown carried by this member of the Territorial Defence, who is also shown wearing the Gelateika uniform. While widely deployed in combat elsewhere in late February 2022, not a single Javelin is known to have been fired during the Battle of Chernihiv, because by the time of their arrival, there were no suitable targets to find. (Artwork by Giorgio Albertini)

Right: During the Battle of Chernihiv, the Ukrainian armed forces deployed a number of anti-tank guided missile systems. This operator from the 16th Battalion, 58th Motorised Brigade is shown preparing his 9K111 Fagot system for action. Notable is his uniform including a civilian parka in black, and trousers of the Gelateika uniform, typical for its MM14 pixel camouflage. (Artwork by Giorgio Albertini)

In 2008, the VKS adopted the Su-34 as its new frontal bomber, aiming to replace the old Su-24Ms. This example, Bort 24, serial number RF81879, was operated by the 2nd Guards Composite Aviation Regiment. The jet was shot down over Chernihiv on 5 March 2022 and the crew ejected, but only the pilot – Major Aleksander Krasnoyartsev survived to become a prisoner of war. The jet is shown as configured at the time it was shot down: armed with eight OFZAB-500 bombs, and a pair of R-73 or R-74 air-to-air missiles for self-defence. (Artwork by Tom Cooper)

This is a reconstruction of the Mi-8MT with the serial number 135, assigned to the 11th Army Aviation Brigade, ZSU. On 3 March 2022, while underway over the Novaya Basan area, it was shot down by air defence systems of the Russian ground forces. One crew-member was killed, while two were wounded and captured, and – in April 2022 – exchanged for the Russian Su-34 pilot Major Krasnoyarcev. The helicopter is shown in typical armament configuration of this period, including B-8 pods for 80mm unguided rockets on outboard outrigger, and a UPK-23 pod for 23mm GSh-23 autocannon on the inboard outrigger. The inscription on the fin reads 'Za Babu Veru!' ('For Old Woman Vera') in not the finest Ukrainian. (Artwork by Luca Canossa)

As of February 2022, Ukraine was still in the process of receiving two batches of Turkish-made Bayraktar TB.2 unmanned combat aerial vehicles. They proved highly effective during the first few days of the Russian invasion, but began suffering losses once the VSRF powered up its air defences, and then combined these into an effective integrated air defence system, covering all of the frontlines. The example with serial number T51, Bort 402 saw action over Chernihiv Oblast, and is known to have been shot down by Russian air defences in early March 2022. (Artwork by Goran Sudar)

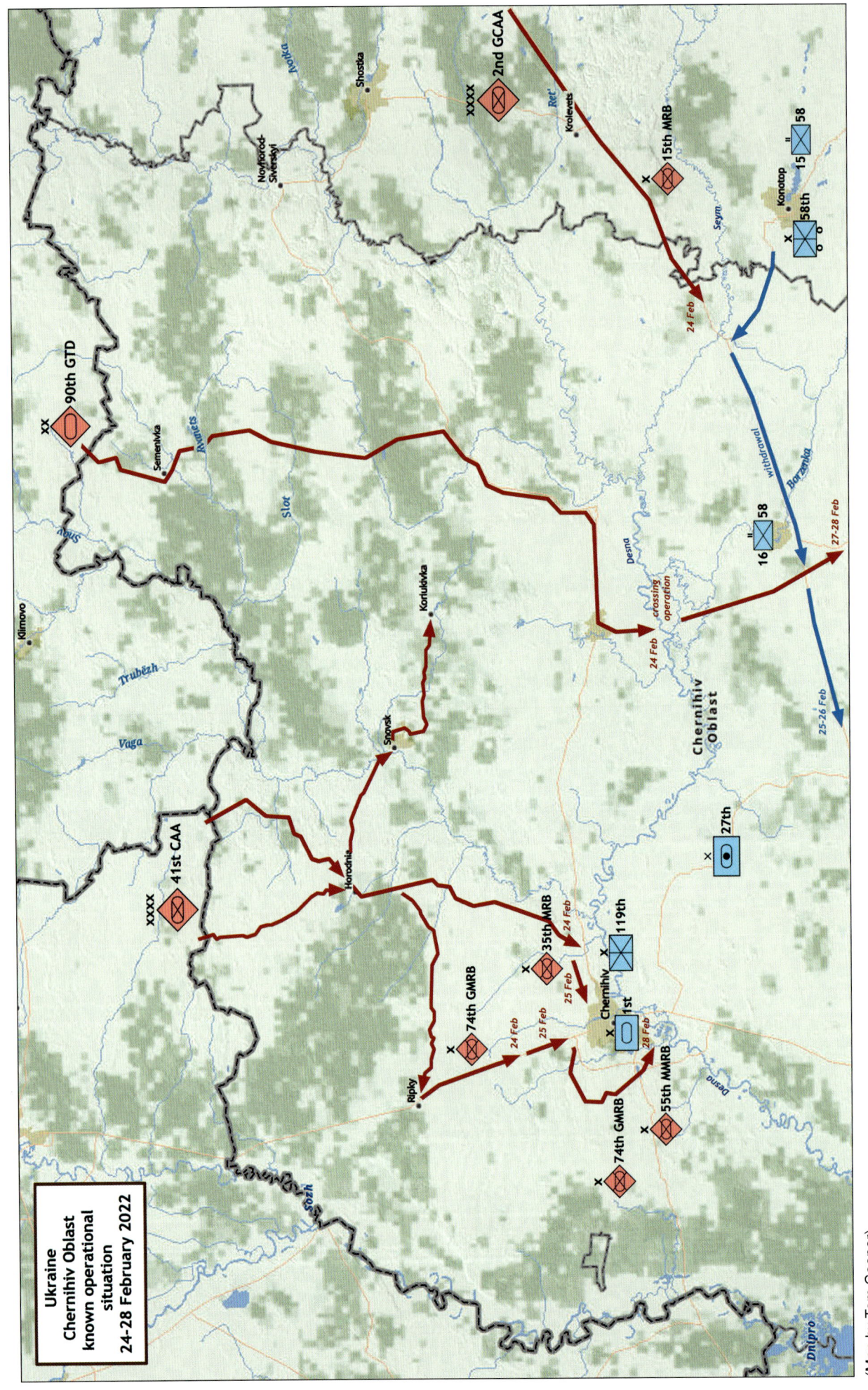

they no longer dared to break through our roadblock so aggressively, and that's why they only hit from afar'.[2]

The two leading Russian T-72s survived the ambush and continued along the M01 in a northern direction, nevertheless. One of them hit a mine, threw off a track and was abandoned by the crew, but the second continued firing at Ukrainian infantry with its coaxial machine gun. Major Khrebtov then brought in both of his T-64BVs and opened fire: the first APFSDS round hit the T-72 on the turret ring, jamming its mount. Moments later, the Russian tank was hit by a HEAT round that blew the turret away. The battle of Kolychivka was thus over, though by then a company of the 15th Battalion was left with only two out of the original 10 BRDMs in operational condition, and all the mortar tubes unserviceable due to constant firing.[3]

The Fall of Lukashivka

Despite the failure to secure Kolychivka, Ryzhkov continued to search for a way to complete the encirclement of Chernihiv. Like in the case of the Sparta position, he decided to flank the Ukrainians in Kolychivka well to the south, through a push on the villages of Sloboda, Lukashivka and Budy, with the aim of reaching Baklanova Muravika, which dominated the P56 Highway, the last road into Chernihiv still under the control of the ZSU. For this effort, Ryzhkov concentrated all of his remaining forces: a total of about 36 T-72s and about 70 BMP-2s, BTR-82As, and MT-LBs.

For their part, the Ukrainians did not try to defend Sloboda, but held Lukashivka with a small task force including about 40 troops with two 9K111 Fagot (ASCC/NATO reporting name 'AT-4 Spigot') ATGMs from the 16th Battalion, 58th Motorised Brigade, and 120 troops from the 2nd Company, 21st Independent Rifle Battalion of the Territorial Defence (with two foreign-made anti-tank grenade launchers). A day later, the Ukrainians were reinforced by two T-64s from the 1st Tank Brigade, both of which were in poor technical condition (indeed, one could not move due to the failure of its battery, while the other had a faulty charging system) and three or four BRDM-2s from the 58th Motorised Brigade. Thanks to information from the local population, the ZSU knew about the large concentration of the Russians in the Yahidne area, and their garrison in Lukashivka expected an enemy attack from the south. Therefore, the troops of the 58th took up positions in the southern outskirts of the village, while those of the Territorial Defence occupied the northern side.

An FGM-148 Javelin in the hands of the defender of Chernihiv, March 2022. (Author's collection)

A T-64BV tank of the 1st Tank Brigade destroyed in battle in Lukashivka, seen in summer 2022. (V.Kozhmal via M.Zhirohov)

Early on 9 March, the Russians moved into Sloboda only to find it not occupied by the ZSU. Therefore, they turned north and assaulted in the direction of Lukashivka. Around 07.00hrs, about a company of T-72Bs of the 74th GMRB, followed by BMP-2s of the 90th Tank Division assaulted from multiple directions, resulting in three only indirectly related clashes: one on the 'left flank' of the ZSU position, the other on the 'right flank', and one for the farm south of Lukashivka, which was held by troops of the 2nd Company, 21st Battalion. Hopelessly outnumbered and immobilised already before the fighting began, the two T-64s were destroyed right at the start of the assault, although their crews seem to have survived: in turn, they managed to fire only two shells. Next, one of the Ukrainian BRDM-2s was hit, together with a ZIL truck carrying a stock of ATGMs.

Pushing forward, the Russians then overwhelmed the defenders of the farm: the Ukrainians fought back from buildings and a small ditch circling the perimeter, but began suffering losses to 30mm autocannon of the Russian IFVs. While brothers Roman and Leonid Butisin – ethnic Russian soldiers of the 58th – managed to destroy one BMP-2, both were killed in return. Volodymyr Haidaichuk from the 21st Battalion, was wounded by a tank round, and dragged into the farm's chicken coup by his comrades, only to be buried under falling rubble, dug out, and buried again as additional shells obliterated the building. Miraculously, he survived and was carried away by one of the tank crews. A group of about 60 surviving Ukrainians attempted to escape over the field north of the farm but ran into a column of Russian trucks that had apparently lost its direction. In a firefight at short range, both the commander of the 2nd Company and several Russians were killed. Fortunately for the remaining Ukrainians, a heavy snowfall then blanketed the battlefield, enabling the majority of survivors to escape in the direction of Baklanova Muravika. By then, about 20 ZSU officers and other ranks had been killed, several taken prisoner (one of them was exchanged only in 2025), while a number of scattered troops were hidden by the local civilians: some made it to the friendly lines, but a few were caught by the Russians and summarily executed. A group of nine captives was tortured by the commander of the 74th GMRB's battalion tactical group that led the assault on Lukashivka, then loaded into an MT-LB that was supposed to take them to the rear. To their good fortune, while underway to Ivanivka, the vehicle hit a mine and lost a track, enabling them to escape. When the Russian crew trapped inside the burning vehicle cried for help, they closed the vehicle's hatches on them.

Above: Possible target of the brothers Butusin: a destroyed Russian BMP-2 in Lukashivka. (Author's collection)

Left: Alley of memory of Ukrainian soldiers who died in the defence of Lukashivka, 2024. (Author's collection)

Budy

As much as securing Kolychivka was a success, the action of 9 March marked the high point of the Russian advance in the Chernihiv area, and the closest they came to encircling the city. When Ryzhkov sent a reconnaissance group including two T-72Bs to check the situation in Baklanova Muravivka – a village constructed on a low but dominating elevation – one of the tanks was hit by a Skif guided anti-tank missile (also known as the Stugna-P), while the rest of the group retreated. No direct assault followed, instead, the village – now held by elements of the 16th Battalion, 58th Motorised Brigade, supported by numerous MT-12 Rapira 100mm towed anti-tank guns – was periodically subjected to volleys from BM-21 and BM-27 multiple rocket launchers, and air strikes.

Still under pressure to effect an encirclement of Chernihiv, Ryzhkov did launch one additional assault on Budy, 15 kilometres further south. Following a five-hour-long artillery preparation, on 17 March 2022, several T-72s, supported by a number of BMP-2s, attacked. By then, the Ukrainian positions were already well protected by a deep minefield, ATGMs, and artillery. Thus, the Russians abandoned their assault as soon as the crew of the leading BMP-2 detected the presence of mines ahead of them.

The following morning, the Russians heavily shelled the minefield. This enabled an assault group of the 74th Guards Motor Rifle Brigade to punch through and approach Buda, only to run into Skifs again. One tank was hit, caught fire and then its ammunition detonated, instantly killing two of the crew. The third was blown out of the turret and died after reaching a friendly position. The second tank stopped and started shooting at Ukrainian positions but then hit a mine while resuming the advance. The weak protection of the T-72B's lower hull sealed its fate. Pushing onwards, the rest of the assault group managed to enter Budy and reach the centre of the village, but this was only a part of the Ukrainian plan. The troops of the 16th Battalion fell back while calling in a pre-registered strike by BM-27 multiple rocket launchers of the 27th Rocket Brigade. This hit the Russians so heavily, that the shaken survivors fled back to Sloboda. The 58th Motorised Brigade then returned to Budy, recovered its positions and set up a new minefield. From that point onwards, Ryzhkov limited the pressure on the village to air strikes, the most massive of which were flown on 25, 26 and 27 March 2022.

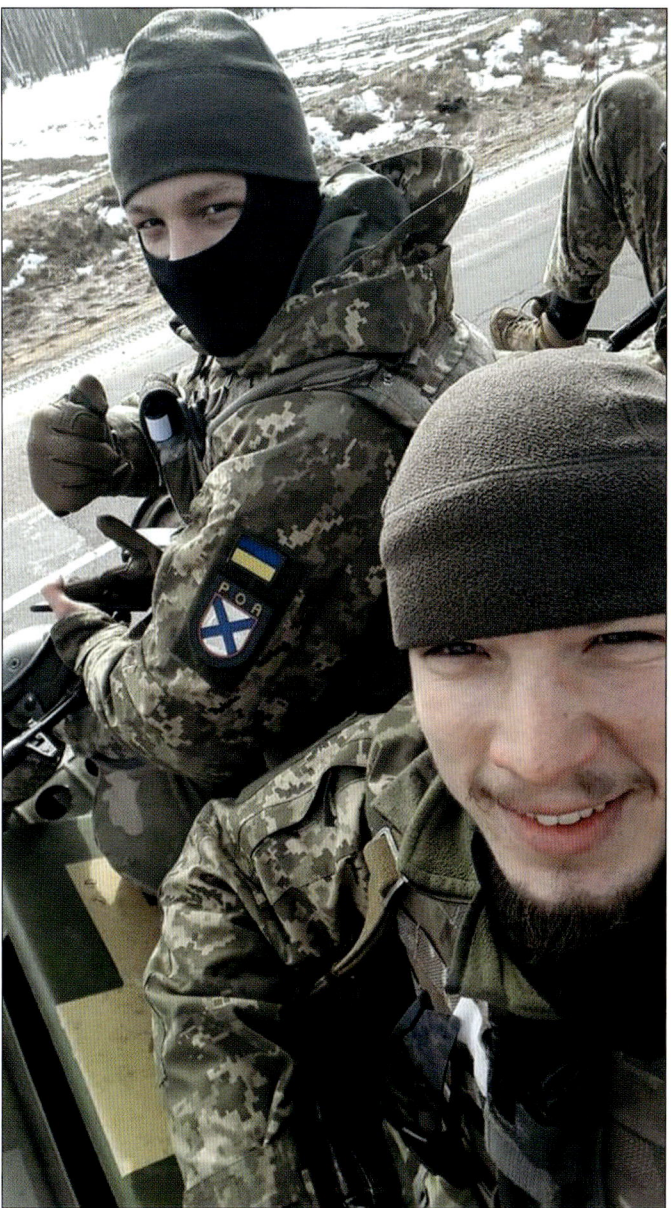

Brothers Roman and Leonid Butusin, while serving in the ZSU. Their family hailed from Vladivostok, and Oleg volunteered to fight against the Russian invasion in 2014. Following the liberation of Chernihiv Oblast, on 8 July 2023, both were posthumously awarded the title the Hero of Ukraine with the Golden Star. (Author's collection)

A battery of 2S1 self-propelled howitzers of the 58th Motorised Brigade firing at the enemy, Chernihiv region, March 2022. (Author's collection)

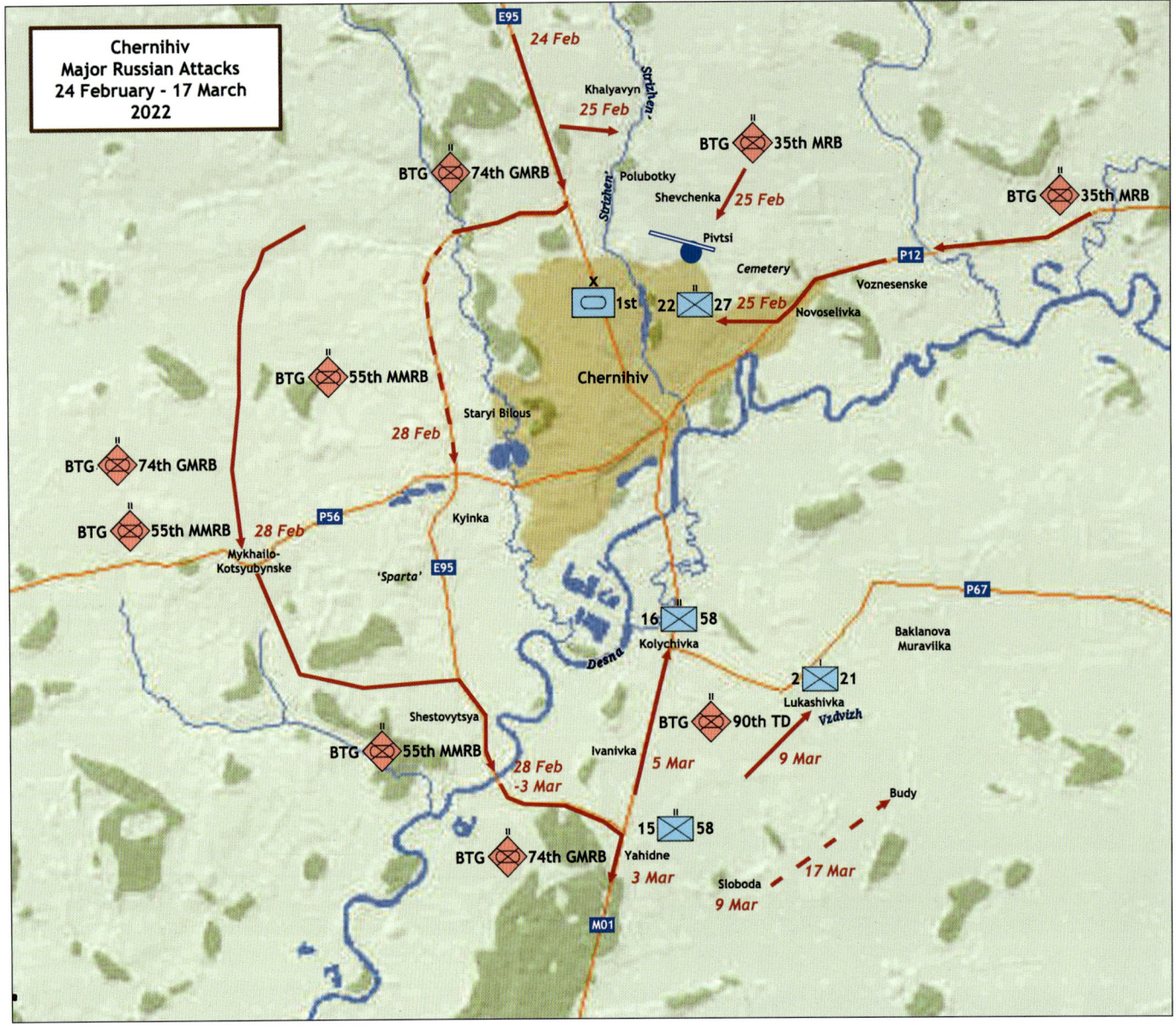
(Map by Tom Cooper)

Novoselivka

By mid-March, the fighting was not only raging south of Chernihiv, but also in its north-eastern suburbs. There, the focus of both sides became the suburban village of Novoselivka and its immediate neighbourhood.

On 24 February, the Operational Command North of the ZSU directed elements of the 21st Independent Rifle Battalion of the Territorial Defence, and the 134th Independent Security Battalion to this place. The troops assumed control around noon, and then used earth-moving machinery to dig a 200-metre-long trench on the dominating elevation – a low hill north of the Ukrnafta petrol station positioned at the end of the P12 Highway. While this was going on, Ukrainian patrols underway on the northern approaches to the village encountered the approaching enemy and exchanged fire with assault rifles. Around 14.00hrs, as the troops closer to Novoselivka were still in the process of constructing their primary position, the site was subjected to Russian artillery fire. Eventually, the Russians withdrew and the Ukrainians not only took up positions on either side of the road but also constructed additional fortifications.

Further east, the Ukrainians constructed a number of additional trenches either side of the P12 Highway. One of these was protecting Voznesenske, a large village held by 15 ZSU troops: they were rotated in and out every three to four days. Finally, inside Novoselivka, the Ukrainians occupied a room in the dormitory of the Siverianka garment factory.

Except for the passage of 35th MRB's two column during the failed forays into Chernihiv on 26 February, the Novoselivka area saw no fighting for the next week, but both sides continued bringing reinforcements to this area. Then, in early March, the Russians began chaotically shelling both Chernihiv and the village, which was also subjected to attacks by the Spetsnaz – the special operation troops of the Main Intelligence Directorate of the General Staff (*Glavnoye Razvedyatelnoye Upravleniye*, GRU). By mid-March, the number of the Russian troops, and their equipment deployed north of Novoselivka were clearly outmatching those of the Ukrainians, and the GRU and VSRF began increasing their pressure. At 04.00hrs on 16 March 2022, Ryzhkov's forces then launched their assault. A massive artillery barrage almost levelled to the ground the forest plantations north of the village, and then the T-72Bs appeared: one of them scored a direct hit on a house atop of the hill, demolishing it and setting its remnants afire. Next, at least two groups of Spetsnaz attacked the Ukrainians from the rear. Oleksandr Antonenko (who returned during one of the exchanges later in 2022), recalled that immediately after the artillery barrage, a group of 16 Russian special

A view from the north towards Novoselivka. Visible on the right side is the low elevation atop of which the Ukrainians constructed their main defence position, the point for which the battles were to rage all through March 2022. (Author's collection)

forces operators wearing night vision goggles and body armour, and armed with assault rifles equipped with silencers, approached from the direction of the village of Tovstolis and jumped into the trench he was defending. They overpowered the small Ukrainian garrison, killing four and forcing the survivors to withdraw. An officer of the 1st Tank Brigade confirmed that the Russians lost up to 10 killed, and four were captured. However, he also confirmed that the Ukrainians were forced to abandon their position and lost not only four killed but also one captured (obviously, this was Antonenko).[4]

Having lost the position dominating Novoselivka, the ZSU then withdrew from Voznesenske as well: indeed, it fell back for about 3,000 metres to the west. A new defence line was constructed at the Yatsevo Cemetery, and along the ski base (officially the Sports Ski Base of the Olympic Reserve of Ukraine), further south-west. Constructed in 1977, on the northern fringe of Chernihiv, this facility was used for Ukrainian biathlon races: now it became the scene of the next major battle.

Held by 58 lightly-armed troops of the ZSU, this position came under attack by the Russian Spetsnaz on 22 March: while 50 Ukrainians withdrew to avoid being surrounded, eight were cut off while hiding inside the basement of a factory building south of the cemetery. The commander of the 3rd Battalion, 1st Tank Brigade decided to deploy his meagre reserve and recover the troops: 20 soldiers and a single BMP-2. Much to everybody's surprise, almost as soon as the Ukrainians moved out, the Russians retreated. Indeed, they left one intact BMP-2 and a Tigr-M infantry mobility vehicle behind. With this, the Russians were forced away from Chernihiv in this area as well.

According to official Ukrainian figures, although the fighting in the Novoselivka area remained relatively limited in scope, about 700 Russians were killed and twice as many wounded. The VSRF also lost more than 30 armoured vehicles, four BM-21s, two BM-27s, 10 self-propelled artillery pieces and one T-72B. The Ukrainians reportedly lost up to 100 killed and 300–400 wounded, while four were captured.[5]

A gunner of the Ukrainian Army with his 9K111 Fagot guided anti-tank system, seen during the battle in one of the taller buildings in Chernihiv. (Author's collection)

A soldier of either the 119th Territorial Defence Brigade or the 21st Rifle Battalion seen in the Chernihiv area in spring of 2022. (Author's collection)

6
THE SIEGE

By the time of the Russian attempt to secure Budy, Vladimir Putin's entire plan for a quick invasion of the Ukraine – what he termed a 'Special Military Operation' – was falling apart. The part of the 90th Tank Division that crossed the Desna River did manage to join the 2nd GCAA, and the two then pushed into Bobrovytsya and Brovary. However, they ran into a determined Ukrainian advance and were beaten back with heavy losses. While soft ground limited all the Russian military manoeuvring to the roads, raiding parties of the ZSU continued ambushing the VSRF's logistic connections anywhere between Ripky, north of Chernihiv, and Sumy, and causing massive losses. Not only the 41st CAA, but also the 2nd GCAA, and the 1st Guards Tank Army all lost their offensive capabilities. As a consequence, the Russians not only failed to encircle Chernihiv, but also to reach and cut off Kyiv from the east, and then lost the initiative. Nevertheless, constantly pressed by Putin, Ryzhkov was left with few options but to continue trying to find a way to squeeze the now de facto besieged city.

Random Shelling
Unable to actually enter Chernihiv, Ryzhkov and his commanders were quick in subjecting the city to largely pointless artillery attacks, and then air strikes. The first such case was recorded in the afternoon of 26 February, when a volley of rockets from BM-21s hit several residential buildings in Belova Street. Later the same day, the regional hospital was also damaged by artillery shells. At 14.30hrs on 27 February, six residential buildings in Magistarska Street were damaged, as was the Children's Dental Clinic and the Kotsiubynsky Library. Around 17.40hrs, the Chernihiv Regional Youth Centre – a historical monument erected in 1938 – was damaged by a missile strike.[1]

On 28 February, the artillery of the 41st CAA commenced large-scale, indiscriminate bombardment of the city. At 02.45 in the morning, a residential building in the centre was set afire, while around 12.00hrs the Epicenter supermarket was shelled and completely burned out.

On 1 March, the Russians occupants rocketed several residential areas, including the Masany neighbourhood and Myru Avenue, with BM-21s. A day later, around 12.30hrs, they hit the Chernihiv district hospital, badly damaging the maternity and covid departments. Dozens of nearby residential buildings were damaged, with windows and doors smashed, roofs torn off, walls and administrative buildings damaged, including the district police station. In addition, two rockets hit the Bobrovytsia neighbourhood. On 3 March, around 08.10hrs, the Russians hit an oil depot within the compound of the Aistra works, causing a total of about 5,000 tons of diesel fuel to burn out.

Around 12.00hrs of 3 March 2022, Su-34 fighter-bombers of the Russian Air and Space Forces (VKS) released eight bombs upon a residential area between Vlacheslava Chornovila and Krukhova streets – a place with no military presence whatsoever. At least 47 civilians were killed and 18 wounded. The same day, the Russians also destroyed the Schools No. 18 and No. 21, where at least eight members of the Territorial Defence – which was using the basement as a bomb shelter – were killed. Another five were murdered when a private home outside the School No. 21 was destroyed.[2]

A hot building: the Epicenter supermarket afire on 28 February 2022. (Author's collection)

The first minutes after the Russian airstrike on houses near Chornovola Street on 3 March 2022. (Author's collection)

Policeman Evgeny Polguy arrived on Chornovila Street immediately after this attack: 'When I saw these people, the bodies that were lying, and these terrible screams. There was only anger, like all our people'. A group of people was hit while standing in a line in front of the local pharmacy: 'The woman was lying near a tree, they ran up and checked her, but she was already without signs of life. Her body parts were cut. Another woman was lying near the car, but she was also without signs of life…'

Russian Air Power
While the Ukrainian Air Force & Air Defence Force remained largely uninvolved, the VKS was deployed massively during the siege of Chernihiv. Its primary combat aircraft active in this area were Su-34s forward-deployed at Seshcha and Shatalovo Air Bases (ABs) in the Bryansk Region of the Russian Federation, and Su-25s forward-deployed at Luninets AB in southern Belarus. The Russian aircraft were primarily deploying conventional, free-fall 250kg and 500kg bombs. A small number of precision guided munitions were deployed as well. Helicopter operations by Mi-24s deployed at Seshcha AB, and Ka-52 and Mi-8s deployed at Zyabrovka AB (south-eastern Belarus) were hampered by bad weather. Russian helicopters were primarily deploying unguided 80mm rockets from B-8 pods.

Ukrainian air defences were very limited, and included the Anti-Aircraft Missile and Artillery Divisions of the 1st Tank Brigade and the 58th Motorised Brigade. These included 9K35 Strela-10 self-propelled, infrared homing systems mounted on MT-LB chassis' and Tunguska tracked self-propelled air defence systems. The 134th

One of the few FIM-82 Stinger MANPADs that reached Chernihiv after the siege began. (Author's collection)

Battalion of the Operational Command North also had a number of infrared homing 9K38 Igla ('SA-7 Grail') MANPADs. Later during the siege, a small number of US-made FIM-92 Stinger MANPADs reached Chernihiv: they were distributed to, and deployed by the 1st Tank Brigade and the 105th Border Guard Detachment – the latter of which also operated two Soviet-era ZU-23-2 towed 23mm guns. Inside the city, a number of MANPAD teams and a few ZU-23-2 guns were deployed, primarily in fixed positions, like high-rise buildings or natural elevations, but there were a few mobile teams as well.

The continuously worsening tactical situation on the ground eventually prompted the headquarters of the 41st CAA to demand more intensive air support. The OSK West reacted enthusiastically, however, the combination of bad weather, their poor tactical training, and lack of all-weather combat capabilities of their aircraft and weaponry forced the VKS crews to repeatedly use the same ingress routes and regularly descend under the cover, thus exposing themselves to nearly all types of air defence weaponry in the Ukrainian arsenal. This became particularly obvious on 5 March, when the Russians suffered an entire series of losses.

First, a Su-25 was hit by anti-aircraft gunners of the 1st Tank Brigade and crashed in the marshy terrain outside Budy. The wreckage was never found. Around 11.30hrs, a pair of Su-34s from the 2nd Composite Aviation Regiment descended underneath the clouds to strike a base of the Chernihiv Border Guard Detachment in Chernihiv. The Guards were some of the first units to receive US-made FIM-82 Stinger MANPADs: one of these hit the jet piloted by Major Konstantin Krasnoyarstsev, with Major Konstantin Krivopavlov as weapons systems officer. The badly damaged Su-34 attempted to limp back towards the territory held by the Russian forces, but was then hit by ZU-23-2 anti-aircraft guns and DShKM 12.7mm heavy machine guns, both operated by the Border Guards. At that point in time, the crew activated their emergency escape system. Major Kryvopavlov, was killed during the ejection, while the pilot, Major Krasoyartsev, descended under a parachute in lightly wounded condition. On the ground, while trying to evade the capture, he shot a civilian but was arrested shortly after. The Su-34 crashed into a private home, and subsequently, three unexploded OFZAB-500 napalm bombs were found at the crash site.[3]

Later the same day, around 17.30hrs a pair of Su-34s of the 2nd Composite Aviation Regiment, VKS, was attacking positions of the 58th Motorised Brigade in the Hrabivka area, about 15 kilometres south of Budy. The opportunity was exploited by a MANPADS team of the 58th to fire a single Igla-1. Although the targeted jet – Bort 26, registration RF-81864 – released flare decoys, the weapon hit its rear, causing it to flip out of control.[4] The crew, including pilot Major Ravil Romanovich Gattarov, and weapons systems officer Major Dmytro Runov, ejected too late: Gatarov's body was found shortly after, while Runov went missing: only his helmet was ever found.[5]

Relentless Bombardment

Around 19.00hrs of 6 March, a private house on Desnyaka Street was hit by two shells, killing a mother and her 20-year-old daughter. In the evening, there was also an artillery shelling of a four-story building in Chernihiv, which was hit by two shells. The roof was completely smashed, the fourth-floor apartments were heavily damaged, and windows in all or almost all apartments were blown out. After 19.00 in Chernihiv, Schools No.10, 19, and 20 were

Above: The remains of the Su-34 shot down over Chernihiv on 5 March 2022. (Author's collection)

Left: An unexploded OFZAB-500 bomb, dropped by the VKS on Chernihiv, seen in March 2022. (Author's collection)

The fate of the Su-34 crew shot down by a MANPAD on 5 March 2022 over Chernihiv. (Author's collection)

shelled, and a private house was damaged. School No. 19 caught fire and was heavily damaged as a result of a shell hit on the roof of the building. According to the spokesperson for the Main Directorate of the State Emergency Service, one person was injured. The Kazan Church also came under fire, with the fence destroyed and the walls of the building badly damaged by overpressure. The house opposite the church had its roof destroyed.

On 8 March, combat aircraft of the VKS dropped a number of FAB-500 500kg bombs on Chernihiv. The artillery then hit a 14-story building in General Belov Street. During the night from 9 to 10 March, the Russians shelled one of the central streets of Chernihiv, and around 23:30 hit a group of people leaving the regional centre: four were killed and four wounded. Around 00.30hrs of 11 March, the aviation carried out an air strike on the Yuri Gagarin Stadium: several bombs missed, badly damaging the historical building of the Vasyl Tarnovsky Museum of Ukrainian Antiquities, a nineteenth-century architectural monument.[6] On the same day, a dormitory in the Bobrovytsia neighbourhood of Chernihiv was shelled, as were residential buildings in the Sherstyanka neighbourhood.

Helicopters of the Ukrainian Army Aviation were also active over Chernihiv Oblast that day. A pair of Mi-8s from the 11th Brigade, home-based in Kherson, was attacking Russian positions in the Nova Basan area, in the Nizhyn District, when one of them was hit by a Tor-M2 self-propelled air defence system (ASCC/NATO reporting name 'SA-15 Gauntlet'). One of three crewmembers, Captain Volodymyr Skliar, was killed (he was posthumously promoted to major and awarded the Order of Bohdan Khmelnytsky, III degree), while the other two, Captain Oleksiy Chyzh and Captain Ivan Pepelashko, were taken prisoners.[7]

On 11 March 2022, anti-aircraft crews of the 1st Tank Brigade claimed a Russian Sukhoi fighter-bomber as hit over Chernihiv. Reportedly, the jet crashed somewhere north of the city, in the territory under the temporary control of the VSRF, its wreckage was never found. Around 02.00hrs on 12 March, a Russian Iskander ballistic missile destroyed the Hotel Ukraine in downtown Chernihiv. Later on, Russian television claimed this was a base of 'US mercenaries': actually, the hotel was completely empty, as evidenced by the absence of rescue operations after the missile strike. During the following night, the VKS flew three air strikes on Chernihiv, damaging several high-rise buildings. Five days later, while clearing the wreckage, the rescuers found the bodies of a family of five inside, including three children between three and 12 years old.

It is possible that the Ukrainian air force launched an intercept attempt during a similar Russian air strike flown on 15 March. However, the involved MiG-29 then crashed outside Novyi Bykiv. According to local residents, the pilot successfully ejected and later reached the territory controlled by the Ukrainian Defence Forces.

The Russians continued bombing the city through 13 and 14 March, when the National University of Chernihiv Polytechnic was hit, an air raid destroyed one of the pumping stations supplying water to the city, and a shell hit the administrative building of Chernihivgaz JSC. Overall, 10 civilians were killed on 14 March 2022 alone. In turn, the Ukrainian defenders claimed two additional jets of the VKS as shot down: one on 13th and the other on 14 March. In the latter case, the fighter-bomber was felled by a FIM-82 Stinger MANPAD operated by Sergeant Vladyslav Mohylnyi: he claimed to have hit one of two jets underway over the village of Tovstolis. No confirmation was available until the Russians withdrew, when the wreckage was found outside Yatseve Cemetery.[8]

The Hotel Ukraine in the centre of Chernihiv, destroyed by a Russian Iskander ballistic missile on 12 March 2022. (Author's collection)

Trophies of the Ukrainian Armed Forces: the flight helmets of Russian pilots shot down in Chernihiv and its surroundings. (Author's collection)

The flight jacket of a Russian pilot shot down in the Chernihiv region. (Author's collection)

On 16 March, around 10.00hrs, Russian Msta-S self-propelled howitzers shelled a line of people waiting to buy bread from the Soyuz store in the Dotsenko Street, killing 14.[9] Later the same day, they also hit an apartment building on Ivan Mazepa Street and, around 20.00hrs, a two-story building where two women and a child were killed. The artillerists of the 41st CAA were more successful elsewhere during that day, when a volley from BM-21 MLRS struck the position of a Strela-10 self-propelled anti-aircraft vehicle of the 1st Tank Brigade: the vehicle was destroyed and two of its crew were killed.

Around 10.00hrs of 17 March, the Russians struck Chernihiv with a volley of rockets from a BM-27 system, killing four people with cluster bomblets that hit Myra Avenue near the Gradetsky Hotel. Probably the worst type of attacks were random rocketing by BM-27 multiple rocket launchers, which often saw the deployment of cluster bomb ammunition. By this time, damage to the water-supply system had reached such proportions that it was dysfunctional in most of the city, and the residents began taking water from the rivers Stryzhen and Desna, and from makeshift wells directly from under the asphalt. The authorities attempted to organise the supply of drinking water centrally, but the Russians reacted by intentionally and repeatedly targeting the resulting crowds. The Russian artillery also shelled the vehicle fleet of municipal utilities in Chernihiv, destroying numerous ATP-2528s.

On 18 March, a house in Rokosovskogo Street caught fire after shelling, and two dormitories in the south-western part of Chernihiv were also damaged; 11 were injured. A day later, the Russian artillery shelled the western part of Chernihiv, causing three large fires: in a warehouse for petrol and lubricants, a plastic goods factory, and City Hospital No.2. Two days later, the residential quarter in Tychynya Street was damaged as a result of shelling, while on 23 March, a single shell hit the engine room of a beer-production plant, damaging the

A direct hit into a residential building of Chernihiv. (Author's collection)

main ammonia pipeline and shattering one tank. Later the same day, the Russians shelled a minibus distributing humanitarian supplies and evacuating residents, and killed its volunteer driver.

Last Bridges

When even Putin was forced into the realisation that the 41st CAA was unable to secure Chernihiv, nor to at least encircle and squeeze its defenders, the OSK West and Ryzhkov received a new order. Therefore, the shelling of the city was intensified. With the majority of attacks being undertaken based on tips from local informants of the Russian intelligence services, and the OSK West next to never cross-examining the information in question, the number of atrocities against civilians continued increasing.

As the ZSU garrison continued to resist, but also to evacuate a growing number of residents across the bridge carrying the P67 Highway across the Desna River south of Chernihiv – while, of course, using the same avenue of communication to keep its troops supplied – the Russians increased the pressure. First, the VKS sought to suppress the Ukrainian air defences through searching for these and targeting them with air strikes. Undertaken on 20 March, the operation had limited results, but a pair of Su-34s did manage to find a single Tunguska self-propelled anti-aircraft system of the 1st Tank Brigade and destroy it with free-fall bombs. In another case, Colonel Khoda recalled a pair of Su-34s that misidentified one of 1st Tank's Brigade T-64s for an air defence vehicle, and bombing a single tank with eight FAB-500M-62 500kg bombs, killing the crew.

Concluding the situation to be safe enough, between 23.15 and 23.25hrs of 22 March, the VKS then launched it strike on the bridge carrying the P67 across the Desna: two Sukhoi Su-34 light bombers were involved and, according to eyewitnesses, the jets made two passes to deploy guided air-to-ground missiles (probably Kh-29; ASCC/NATO reporting name 'AS-14 Kedge') to demolish their target. With this blow, the garrison was deprived of its primary logistic link: the sole fixed connection over the river became a small bridge for pedestrians, which was mainly used to evacuate the local residents. This was targeted next: starting from 23 March, the Russians subjected it to fire from 120mm mortars. After the first hit, all traffic was stopped: Chernihiv was now physically cut off from the rest of Ukraine.

Throughout the night from 24 to 25 March, the VKS and the Russian artillery hit several points around the city, killing two and wounding at least one person. Determined to save as many lives as possible, General Nikolyuk and Colonel Bryzhynsky continued the evacuation of civilians. Indeed, they contacted Ryzhkov and arranged a 'humanitarian corridor' for this purpose: this was to enable as many civilians as possible to cross the Desna River by boats. Correspondingly, around 16.50hrs of 25 March, dozens of civilians gathered at the predetermined spot – which soon came under the observation of a Russian reconnaissance UAV. Fifteen minutes later, the area was targeted by a volley from BM-27 MLRS, followed by 122mm artillery, and then 120mm mortars. The number of victims remains unknown.[10] Elsewhere the same day, one woman was killed when a volley from BM-21s hit a multi-storey building in Dotsenko Street.

On 26 March, the Russians damaged two schools and several residential buildings, and hit a civilian car from Ivano-Frankivsk that was carrying humanitarian aid, and the mayor of Ivano-Frankivsk. Two days later, the VSRF shelled residential areas in the northern part of the city, mostly along Myru Avenue, causing

The main road bridge carrying the P67 Highway over the Desna River. It was destroyed by Russian Su-34s late in the evening of 22 March 2022. (Author's collection)

significant damage to numerous buildings and wounding one person. Additionally, a 14-storey building in General Belov Street was hit and two people wounded, and a team of civilian volunteers came under fire outside the city: their vehicle was destroyed, and three people seriously wounded.

During the night from 30 to 31 March, Chernihiv was hit by a particularly powerful artillery strike. Around 01.15hrs, the city centre was hit and the Central Market almost completely demolished, as were the Detsky Mir and Polissia shopping centres, the Main Post Office and the Korolenko Universal Library.[11] Around 11.00hrs, the Russians then shelled five buses that arrived to evacuate civilian residents. One female volunteer was killed and four others wounded. Finally, on 1 April 2022, the Russian military shelled the Chernihiv Centre for Modern Oncology, injuring two employees with shrapnel wounds and another person with concussion. There were 22 patients in the room where the shell hit, including palliative care patients and people after surgery, who could not leave the facility and needed constant medical supervision.

The symbol of unconquered Chernihiv: the wreckage of a BM-27 rocket that crashed into a children's playground. (Author's collection)

Remnants of cluster munitions from BM-27 Uragan MLRS on the streets of Chernihiv after the strike on 17 March 2022. (Author's collection)

THE FRONTLINE BOMBER

Based on the design of the Sukhoi Su-27, the development of what was originally the Su-32, and then Su-34, began in the 1980s, with the aim of replacing not only the old Su-24 frontline bomber, but also the Su-25 ground attack aircraft. The first prototype was completed in 1990, but series production initiated only in 2008. Due to the lack of necessary funding, it was only in 2005 that the Russian Ministry of Defence penned the first contract for delivery of 18 Su-34s: even then, only one was manufactured in 2008, two in 2009, and two in 2010 – all of which were used for testing. In November 2008, a new contract was signed for 32 Su-34s, to be manufactured by the works in Novosibirsk, including two in 2010, six in 2011, 10 in 2012, and 14 in 2013.

Meanwhile, in August 2008, the type made its combat debut during the Russian invasion of Georgia, where single jets of this type were deployed as electronic support aircraft. The Russian Su-34s saw a much larger deployment in Syria, starting with August-September 2015, where they suffered no losses although flying up to 20 percent of the total of over 160,000 known combat sorties recorded by the VKS.

In February 2012, the Ministry of Defence in Moscow signed another contract, this time for 92 aircraft to be delivered by 2020. The works in Novosibirsk worked hard and delivered ahead of the deadline: 18 new Su-34s were manufactured each in 2014 and 2015, and 16 each in 2016 and 2017. Overall, by the end of 2020, the VKS received 129 Su-34s.

Subsequent contracts were much less transparent. In August 2020, Moscow seems to have placed an order for 24 Su-34NVOs: this was a new sub-variant, pending the availability of the fully modernised Su-34. In August 2022, another 76 Su-34NVOs and Su-34Ms were ordered, with delivery due by 2027. As far as is known, eight Su-34NVO were manufactured in 2021, and another 10 in the year after; three batches of two to four bombers were delivered in 2023. Overall, by the end of 2023, the VKS should thus have got 151 to 159 Su-34s.

Four of the pre-production examples and three Su-34s manufactured in series are known to have been written off in training accidents before 24 February 2022, while a staggering 25 have been visually confirmed as shot down in combat over Ukraine by December 2023 alone (including at least one Su-34NVO).

An early Su-34 from series production, seen in VKS service. (MoD Russian Federation)

Table 5: Availability of Su-34s in the Russian VKS as of 24 February 2022

Regiment	Base	Quantity	Known losses during the war in Ukraine
47th Bomber Regiment	Voronezh-Baltimore	24	6
559th Bomber Regiment	Morozovsk, Rostov region	36	2
2nd Guards Composite Aviation Regiment	Chelyabinsk-Shagol	24	3
277th Bomber Regiment	Khurba, Khabarovsk Territory	30	3

7
RADIOACTIVE VACATION

In addition to the city of Chernihiv, another area of high Russian interest in this part of Ukraine was the Exclusion Zone surrounding the former nuclear power plant (NPP) of Chernobyl. Situated on the western bank of the Dnipro River, this was subjected to administrative control of Kyiv, even if mostly being within Chernihiv Oblast.

Quick Work
At the start of the Russian all-out invasion, the Chernobyl NPP was guarded by a battalion of 169 troops of the National Guard, a company of troops from the 80th Airborne Brigade, and a group of sappers. The Ukrainians developed a relatively elaborate plan for the defence of this area, and this envisaged all the bridges being blown up. However, nearly everything went wrong, as recalled by one of the sappers:

> On 23 February 2022, we received combat orders. As part of three groups, we deployed in the area of the village of Cherevach near Chornobyl to prepare for the mining of three road bridges across the Uzh River. The war began at four in the morning of 24 February. We mined bridges under enemy fire. We were the last to leave the area.
>
> There were air strikes on the Chernobyl zone. People panicked and ran away. We were the first to mine the main bridge at the exit from Chernobyl near the village of Cherevach, but we could not blow it up because the evacuation was ongoing. Therefore, we handed it over to the commander of the 2nd Battalion of the 80th Airborne Brigade for destruction: they went higher up the river to mine two more bridges. They were at a great distance from each other, so I decided to split into two groups to save time. My group went to the bridge over the Uzh near the village of Poliske, another group led by Dmytro Shmagail went to prepare and destroy the bridge near the village of Maksymovichi. The bridges were mined when the enemy fired from armoured vehicles and small arms from the opposite side of the river. The last bridge was blown up when the enemy had already crossed it.

One of the Ukrainian officials responsible for monitoring the sarcophagus, recalled:

> On February 24, we woke up at 4 a.m. and started preparing our equipment. We were standing and having breakfast on one of the high-rise buildings when we heard the first explosion... The window offered a beautiful view of the entire Prypiat: on the one hand, you could see the Chornobyl NPP, on the other, the border with Belarus. And it was in that direction that the explosions occurred, I think, five kilometres away. After the

explosions, we immediately heard the roar of rockets flying over Prypiat toward Kyiv.

Eventually, all the bridges were damaged, but not one dropped. The Russians were thus able to quickly move in and secure the huge complex of the former NPP, together with the giant 'sarcophagus' covering the part destroyed during the famous nuclear catastrophe of 1986. The battalion of the National Guard was captured without offering any resistance, while the sappers and troops of the 80th Airborne Brigade rapidly withdrew towards the south.

The VSRF subsequently converted the Chernobyl Exclusion Zone – an area with the highest levels of radioactivity encountered by humans in the open space around the globe – into a major military base. Hundreds of vehicles were temporarily parked there during the following month; many travelled dozens of kilometres off-roads in an area where all traffic had been strictly prohibited since 1986, in order to prevent raising the dust. Unsurprisingly, nearly everything – including vehicles and equipment, but especially troops – was contaminated with radioactive substances. To make matters worse, the commanders of the VSRF units deployed in this area obviously had no trace of clue about how to handle the situation. They also never issued protective equipment to their subordinates, and ignored every single safety rule.

For example, Ukrainian observers that remained in the area recalled that the Russians did not have any personal dosimeters used to detect the radioactivity and record the amount received. Indeed, when one Russian military cook saw them wearing such devices, he started asking questions about it:

We explained it to him, but he didn't understand: why? We began to tell him about radiation, that it is extremely dangerous and in a week he could not hope to have children in the future. Once this Dima said that his knees hurt. Our cook heard these whimpers and said: "These are the first signs. We all have artificial knee joints here, so just wait a little longer". Of course, he didn't believe her. But after such incidents, their attitude to where they are changed.

Despite obvious ignorance of all safety rules, in March 2022, the state-controlled media in Belarus repeatedly reported that the experts from the Belarusian Republic's Scientific and Practical Centre for Radiation Medicine and Human Ecology in Gomel, were regularly visiting the Exclusion Zone and checking the Russian military personnel stationed there. However, the reality was diametrically opposite. The most illustrative of the complete disregard of Russian commanders for the lives of their troops was the situation in the so-called Red Forest. This is an area about 10 square kilometres in size, which took the largest share of the radioactive release during the disaster of 1986. In the process of a particularly complex operation, it was completely buried with hundreds of thousands of tonnes of non-contaminated soil. However, the contamination – and the gamma radiation in particular – remained exceptionally high.

Any earthworks would release particles of radioactive soil into the air, contaminating the air breathed by the Russians with effects harmful for human health. Nevertheless, the VSRF troops constructed numerous earthworks in the Red Forest. Unsurprisingly, all of them received extremely high doses of gamma radiation, but also alpha and beta particles. These were causing not only the redness of the skin, or upsetting the stomach, but damage to the respiratory tract, loss of hair and outright radiation burns. Additional long-term effects included cancer and genetic mutations. Still, the Russians maintained their military base in the area, and this was housing

A Russian BMP-2. In the background is the Chernobyl nuclear power plant. (Author's collection)

several thousands of troops. To make matters worse, on 20 March, many were rotated, further increasing the number of those affected.

The captured Ukrainian National Guardsmen were held as prisoners of war within the Exclusion Zone as well. Indeed, the Russian media attempted to present them as 'partners' and aired videos showing them conducting 'joint patrols', together with Russian troops.

After five weeks of 'guarding' it, the Russians began withdrawing from the Exclusion Zone only on 30 March 2022.[1] An eyewitness recalled that early that day the invaders announced their intention to leave the Chernobyl NPP to the Ukrainian staff, and then forced everybody to sign a paper certifying that they have no claims against the Russian Federation, whatsoever. During the withdrawal, the VSRF troops looted many of the premises, and also took with them all the Ukrainian National Guardsmen: as of early June 2024, 89 of them were still in captivity. The last Russians left this part of Ukraine around 20.00hrs on 31 March 2022.[2]

Slavutych

The last urban centre in Chernihiv Oblast to experience the Russian occupation was the town of Slavutych: a satellite settlement constructed to house some personnel of the Chernobyl NPP, and thus the newest town of Ukraine. Geographically, it was within Chernihiv Oblast, but administratively subjected to Kyiv.

As of 24 February 2022, Slavutych was defended by a 150-strong company of Territorial Defence: its troops were armed with assault rifles, two machine gun, and one MT-LB armoured personnel carrier provided by a nearby unit of the National Guard (which was withdrawn back to Kyiv, a day later). Over the following weeks, the unit received one RPG, several additional machine guns, and even one NLAW anti-tank guided weapon system.

The place was well away from any of the main routes used by the 41st CAA to enter Ukraine and nothing happened until the Russians were forced to withdraw from the cemetery in northern Chernihiv on 23 March 2022. On that day, however, they limited themselves to mortaring Slavutych with 20–25 120mm bombs. Suffering no losses nor damage, on the next morning the local company of Territorial Defence then took up defence positions about seven kilometres outside the town. Shortly after 08.00hrs, as the troops were still in the process of digging trenches, they saw a Russian UAV high in the sky. Attempts to shoot it down by machine guns remained fruitless, and the VSRF then began to mortar their positions, destroying one car and a minibus, even though failing to cause more damage to the personnel other than lightly wounding one.

The following morning a patrol reported the appearance of a column of Russian armoured vehicles about 1,500 metres away. The company promptly retreated back to the outskirts of Slavutych: the centre of its new defence line was in an abandoned clinic, and around the so-called Dry Lake. The Russians did not show up, though: on the contrary, early on 25 March, the Territorials were ordered to hide their weapons and ammunition and return home. Obviously, somebody up the chain of command concluded that due to the lack of anti-tank weapons (the NLAW did not work anymore because its battery was dead), any resistance would have been futile.

Early on 26 March, a column of Russian armoured vehicles entered Slavutych – and was stopped by a large rally of local residents: about 6,000 (the pre-war population was about 25,000) gathered on the central square and unfurled a 100-metre-long flag of Ukraine.[3] The Russians fired into the air in attempt to scatter them, but then withdrew out of the town: as it turned out, they simply waited until the civilians would grow tired and disperse before returning. Indeed, the VSRF then entered the town in the afternoon, and – while formally 'searching for weapons' – its troops began taking away anything they found of any value, primarily mobile telephones. Then, all of a sudden, on the morning of 27 March, the Russians withdrew from Slavutych. By then, three soldiers of the Ukrainian Territorial Defence had been captured and summarily executed, while one died of injuries sustained during an earlier mortar attack. The Armed Forces of Ukraine entered the town on 3 April 2022.

A Russian soldier in the Chernobyl nuclear power plant. (Author's collection)

The public rally in Slavutych, on 26 March 2022. (Author's collection)

CHERNOBYL'S SATELLITE

The decision to construct Slavutych as a new permanent residence for employees of the Chernobyl NPP and their families, was taken on 2 October 1986. The design of the town was completed by December and the construction began almost immediately: it involved architects and constructors from eight republics of the USSR (Armenia, Azerbaijan, Estonia, Georgia, Latvia, Lithuania, Ukraine, and Russia). The town's total built-up area covered 7,500 square kilometres, and it was officially named by a resolution issued on 19 February 1987.

The short history of Slavutych was divided into two periods: from 1987 to 2000 and since December 2000. The town was always heavily dependent on the fate of the Chernobyl NPP. As the activity there constantly reduced, it began losing residents at the rate of 400 per year. When the plant was shut down in 2001, 9,000 residents left almost at once. As of 2021, only about 2,500 remained employed at the Chernobyl NPP. Their primary tasks included maintaining the plant in a safe condition, working on decommissioning, creating infrastructure for spent nuclear fuel and radioactive waste management, and transforming the Exclusion Zone into an environmentally safe system.

Above: Coat of arms of Slavutych. (City Council)

Left: The City Council of Slavutych. (City Council)

8
SUBVERSIVE AND GUERRILLA OPERATIONS

Subversive actions by both local residents and by special forces units became a crucial element of countering the Russians in Chernihiv region. It is known that on the Ukrainian side, soldiers from the 3rd and 8th regiments of the Special Operations Forces (SSO), the 73rd Naval Special Operations Centre named after Kosh Ataman Antin Holovaty, and the 154th Independent Reconnaissance Battalion took part in the fighting. In an interview for this book, one of SSO operators recalled: 'Our task was to reconnoitre the area. We avoided fire contact because we were performing tasks behind enemy lines. We conducted raids in forests, meadows, and settlements, looking for concentrations of enemy equipment and personnel and passing their coordinates to our artillery'.

It was the correction of artillery fire, which was concentrated in Chernihiv and the surrounding area, that was perhaps the most important task for all the special forces, and the most effective. Not only were there the 122mm 2S1 Gvozdika SPG, BM-21 Grad MLRS (brigade artillery of the 1st Tank and 58th Motorized Infantry Brigades) and 152mm Msta-B towed guns from the 44th Artillery Brigade, but also more powerful weapons that were under the operational control of the General Staff of the Armed Forces of Ukraine such as the Tochka-U (ASCC/NATO reporting name 'SS-21 Scarab') operational and tactical missile systems and 203mm Pion SPG. On 25 March 2022, artillery fire destroyed a Russian army ammunition depot in Vyshneve (Ripky village community, Chernihiv district), causing a fire that lasted five hours.

However, the first important action of the SOF should be considered the late night explosion on 26 February 2022 of a train of 51 fuel tanks and five fertiliser cars at the Nyzkivka railway station (between Mena and Snovsk stations), located in the village of Volovyky, Koryukiv district. Officially, it is believed that this is the result of the work of Bayraktar UAV crews or artillery, but according to the author's information, it was the work of special forces. The train itself was commercial, entered Ukraine before the start of the large-scale invasion, and was partially blown up so that the Russians could not use the fuel to refuel their own military equipment.[1]

At the same time, a real hunt for Russian supply convoys began throughout the region. And these actions involved very heterogeneous forces. Unarmed villagers simply blocked the few roads with trees, for example, on 28 February, in Novi Borovychi (Snovska urban community of Koryukivka district), a Russian fuel truck lost control and collided with a tree as a result of a blockage made by local patriots. Territorial Defence fighters caused even more damage, primarily in the areas of Sribne, Nizhyn, and Pryluky.

On 13 March, soldiers and engineers from the Nizhyn group stopped the advance of a column of enemy vehicles. In the course of the battle, they destroyed one KAMAZ truck and one fuel tanker. As a result, two KAMAZ trucks (one of which was carrying an "Igla" MANPADS), an MTU-90 armoured vehicle launched bridge and an IMR-2M engineering barrier vehicle were captured. In this battle, enemy soldiers were also killed, including the head of the engineering service of the 7th Independent Guards Red Banner Order of Suvorov, Kutuzov, Alexander Nevsky Orenburg Tank Cossack Brigade, Captain Nikitin.

In addition, there was a civilian resistance movement, which was coordinated by several structures at once; the ZSU, SBU (*Sluzhba bezpeky Ukrainy*, Security Service of Ukraine) and GUR (*Holovne upravlinnia rozvidky Ministerstva oborony Ukrainy*, Main Directorate of Intelligence of the Ministry of Defence of Ukraine). As Artem, the coordinator of the Movement in the Chernihiv region, said:

A member of the resistance movement was an average inhabitant of the settlement. He is a brave person who, after successful tasks, is also driven by excitement. Sometimes we marvelled at the courage of our people. It deserves respect.

The result of the combat action of a Ukrainian sabotage group in the area of Srybnoye, Chernihiv region. (S. Bibik via M. Zhirokhov)

During the battles in the Chernihiv region, the 19th Missile Brigade of the ZSU deployed many OTR-21 Tochka tactical ballistic missiles. The wreckage of this example was discovered following the Russian withdrawal. (Author's collection)

Fighters of one of the subversive groups active in the Chernihiv district in March 2022. (Author's collection)

Well, an even better member of the resistance movement is one who does not even know that he is involved in this process. This is an example when one of the participants calls his best man, and the best man can see where enemy equipment is standing in the landing. And he does not even understand that he was a participant in this process, and 90% of them, to be honest. The work is structured in such a way that there were several of these people in each settlement, and they, of course, did not know each other at all. This made it possible to create a safe situation for these same people. The second is the verification of information that comes to us from one or another settlement or person.

The main task is the collection of information, transmissions, movement coordinates, the number and location of enemy equipment, the meeting of reconnaissance groups, escorting around the territory.

No one forced anyone, but whenever possible, sabotage was also carried out. People were willingly involved in joint operations to perform specific tasks. And already in the first month, people actually transferred more than 500 coordinates. In fact, they were much more, because we had a certain structure that additionally checked them to be authentic.

According to estimates, somewhere around 200 pieces of equipment were affected. It is not only wheeled, but also partially heavy equipment. Including warehouses with supplies, gas trucks, pontoon crossings. In addition, there were many search tasks.[2]

All these actions were very threatening for the Russians and as a result actually led to a retreat from the northern regions of Ukraine and from Kyiv. The fact is that the Russians based their actions on BTGs. In the classic case, BTGs fight as follows: reconnaissance identifies enemy positions, artillery destroys the identified targets, then the advanced units engage in combat and start a fight, calling for artillery and possibly air support. Subsequent elements of the battle group flank or support the advanced units where success has been achieved, and so on…

However, this was not how the Russians acted. Their battalion tactical groups did not advance in front, but in columns. In form, it was not a classic offensive, but a raid, and it was poorly organised, with little or no reconnaissance or artillery training, and extremely poor logistics.

The Russian BTGs moved forward until they accidentally encountered resistance from the Ukrainian Army. In the classical version, at this point they would have switched from a raid to a conventional offensive. However, the Russian BTGs (at least most of them) were not prepared by their composition to break through the defence of enemy tank and mechanised units. They had too few tanks, infantry, and artillery. Moreover, they were apparently deprived of any elements of intelligence and electronic warfare. Approaching the areas of strong Ukrainian defence, they not only failed to break through them, but did not even ensure that the second echelon BTGs entered the battle. The latter, in turn, fell victim to artillery and ambushes because they had unprotected flanks. The interaction between infantry and tanks in the Ukrainian terrain was insufficient, and the artillery (which was relatively few in number) could not provide fire support on the march, and when they could do so, they simply quickly ran out of ammunition. The first victims of the shelling were the tanker trucks that were part of the BTG. The BTG commanders could not establish the interaction of different types of weapons in such a high dynamic of combat and with such limited resources.

Trophies of the Ukrainian military after the Russian army retreated. (Author's collection)

The Russians' actions were also complicated by natural and climatic factors. Traditionally, most of the territory of northern Ukraine is impassable for heavy equipment during the thaw period following the winter. When planning the operation, the Russian command obviously expected that the network of asphalt roads would be enough for the offensive. However, when the BTGs encountered resistance and were forced to deviate from these roads, their tanks got stuck in the mud. Freezing nights regularly forced the Russian troops to literally live in their combat vehicles, and it turned out they were absolutely not prepared for this. This was compounded by staying in field camps for several winter weeks preceding the invasion, overdue dry rations, and other everyday inconveniences that negatively affected the morale of the soldiers. It is not surprising that commanders looked the other way when their subordinates looted, and sometimes even encouraged this shameful phenomenon. In this way, they tried to prevent the morale of the soldiers from falling. Herein lay another paradox inherent in the Russian army: in any other armed force, looting was a symptom of degradation and loss of combat capability. In the Russian army, on the contrary, looting was considered a proper reward for the risks of military service. Moreover, such behaviour was tolerated by the whole of Russian society: there were countless cases of the wives of Russian soldiers openly boasting of their 'trophies'.

A Russian fuel tanker, which was stopped by local residents blocking a road with trees. (Author's collection)

Ukrainian servicemen against the background of another captured Russian T-72, Chernihiv region, early April 2022 (Author's collection)

At the same time, the Ukrainian military expectedly countered the raiding tactics of the Russian army with a defence based on cities and towns with fortified approaches. This approach proved to be quite effective. A specific confirmation of this is the publication in May 2022 of articles about the use of the Armed Forces of Ukraine in urban combat in two magazines of the Russian Ministry of Defence; *Army Collection* and *Foreign Military Review*.

In general, the tactics of urban combat, both defence and assault, have been developed for a long time, and their principles have not changed since the Second World War. When defending cities, Ukrainians chose a combined method: first, they tried to stop the enemy in the suburbs, and if they managed to break through, they fought fierce battles for each intersection. However, the Russians mostly failed to organise a classic assault on cities (the only exception was Mariupol). The fact is that such an assault requires significant forces, as it involves surrounding the city with two rings. The inner ring creates a perimeter around the city, which ensures relative freedom of movement for the assault forces, while preventing counterattacks by the defenders. The outer ring prevents the penetration of resupply and military supplies into the city. Of course, when talking about a small town, it can be captured by a raid, but with large cities, especially those with strong garrisons, this technique is mostly ineffective. The Russians failed to capture even the smaller regional centres in the north, however, such as Sumy and Chernihiv (each with a population of about 300,000).

As a result, the Russians' actions in Chernihiv, and in the northern regions, including Kyiv, failed. The reason for this is obvious from today's perspective: overestimation of their own forces and a huge underestimation by the Russian command of the Ukrainians' will to fight. Thus, it was supposed to be a quick raid operation that would end with the capture of the Ukrainian capital and the establishment of a collaborationist puppet government. The transition to Plan B, i.e., the attempt to blockade Kyiv, was forced and was not part of the original plans of the Russian command. It soon turned out that there was also a lack of means to realise this intention, and the resistance of the Ukrainian Defence Forces was becoming increasingly strong. In view of this, the Russian military and political leadership decided to abandon its intention to capture Kyiv and focus its efforts on Donbas.

9
RUSSIAN WITHDRAWAL

Catastrophic losses during the first few days of the invasion, followed by a series of tactical defeats of the VSRF in the area northwest and east of Kyiv, followed by the failure of the 41st CAA to effectively besiege Chernihiv, eventually forced Vladimir Putin into the realisation that his forces inside Ukraine were overstretched, and unable to complete their mission. Therefore, he completely changed his strategy for the invasion: abandoning the plot to topple the government in Kyiv and seize all of the country, he ordered a general withdrawal from the three oblasts in the north of the country. The decision to do so was probably taken during or as a result of the meeting of the Security Council of the Russian Federation held on 24 March 2022. In the course of this, Putin discussed the situation with Sergei Shoigu, Valery Gerasimov, Nikolai Patrushev (former Director of the FSB, and then the Secretary of the Security Council of Russia, and one of 'hawks' who played a crucial role in convincing Putin to launch the invasion), and the Director of FSB, Alexander

Bortnikov. The televised section of the meeting showed Putin completely ignoring Bortnikov's report and rebuking Gerasimov's complaints about 'significant' losses in troops and equipment by explaining to him that a loss of 30,000–50,000 men was nothing comparable to what Russia would achieve through its victory. The fact that Petrushev, in the part of the meeting that was shown on the Russian TV, reported that 'everything is prepared' for a general mobilisation, is indicative of the five men already concluding that Russia was in urgent need of downscaling the invasion in order to find the troops necessary to secure at least all of the Luhansk, Donetsk, Zaporizhzhia, and Kherson oblasts.

The logical result was refocusing the aims of the war to the battlefields in the east and south of Ukraine. To find the necessary troops without a mobilisation, Putin ordered a withdrawal from the north. Typically, the task of informing the Russian public – and thus the foreign media, too – about what was actually bad news, fell on Shoigu. On 28 March, he announced that after 'destroying the Ukrainian armed forces' in the Kyiv area, Russia is now about to focus on the 'key objective' of its invasion: the 'liberation of Donbass'. At least some of the Russian media went as far as describe this as a 'good-will gesture'.

Elements of the 90th Tank Division began withdrawing on the same day Shoigu's announcement was aired on Russian TV. The first elements of the division, including about 120 vehicles, travelled along the route from Shevchenkove, via Bobryk, Bervitsa, Stara Basan, Pisky, to Nova Basan. The second, including about 50 vehicles, moved from Nova Basan to Novyi Bykiv. The manoeuvre was covered by vicious artillery barrages on nearby ZSU units, which followed only cautiously. Still, on 1 April, the Ukrainians liberated Nova Basan, finding there several abandoned BTR-82As and at least one dysfunctional T-72B3 – along with dozens of corpses of dead Russian troops.

On the contrary, the withdrawal order caught General Ryzhkov by surprise: at the time, he was still preparing one last attempt to complete the encirclement of Chernihiv. Only hours after this was cancelled, a severe Ukrainian artillery barrage and additional Tochka strikes hit the Shestovytsya crossing site, the positions of the 55th MMRB and the 74th GMRB in Yahidne, and the forward headquarters of the 41st CAA in Vyshneve. The attacks on Shestovytsya proved particularly devastating, because – amongst others – they blew up several local storage sites for VSRF forces deployed south of Desna. As a consequence, Ryzhkov had no means to supply them with fuel anymore. The activity of the Ukrainian special forces behind the Russian lines was growing in intensity as well. On 30 March, these succeeded in blowing up an ammunition depot in the church of Lukashivka: the resulting explosion also destroyed 12 armoured vehicles and an entire mortar battery. The same morning, the 58th Motorised Brigade launched an attack on Sloboda, aiming to encircle Lukashivka and trap the two weak BTGs there. According to Khoda, this operation miscalculated somewhat, though, and the demoralised, freezing, and starving Russians were able to flee from the trap the following night. According to Nikolyuk, they left behind over 70 percent of their equipment while retreating across the Shestovytsya crossing.

The following morning, on 1 April, the 41st CAA commenced its general withdrawal from Chernihiv Oblast. Characteristically, the biggest problem it encountered was the transportation of the property looted from Ukraine. For such purposes, soldiers of the VSRF regularly used stolen civilian vehicles, a number of which were overloaded to the point of breaking down. Dozens were captured or killed while lagging behind their units. Nevertheless, the drive to take away the loot often reached such proportions that the Russians were more concerned about their 'business' than with evacuating tanks and other heavy vehicles. As a result, the ZSU captured huge numbers of tanks, IFVs, trucks, and other equipment. Unsurprisingly, Nikolyuk subsequently claimed that only about 60 percent of VSRF troops and equipment that entered Chernihiv on 24 February were successfully evacuated by the time the entire oblast was liberated, on 5 April 2022.

Local residents greet advancing Ukrainian troops on 1 April 2022. (Ukrainian MOD)

A Russian tank found after the withdrawal of the 90th Tank Division in April 2022. (Author's collection)

A Pantsir-S1 medium-range surface-to-air missile and anti-aircraft artillery system destroyed in the Vyshneve district, Chernihiv region. (Author's collection)

10
CONSEQUENCES

After the Russians withdrew, the Ukrainians found hundreds of abandoned military vehicles, a similar number of corpses of Russian soldiers, huge amounts of equipment and gear, and large-scale destruction of the towns and villages northwest of Kyiv; for example, Irpin and Bucha were two-thirds destroyed and uninhabitable. At least as shocking were massacres of civilians: as of May 2022, 432 bodies of civilians murdered by the Russians in Chernihiv Oblast were found. Another 609 people were wounded.[1] Of course, Moscow immediately denied any responsibility for the killing of civilians. At most, it explained that these were massacred by the Ukrainian Army.

Russian activities in the occupied villages of the Chernihiv region have now become known. The tragedy of the village of Yahidne, where the occupiers entered on 3 March and locked all 350 residents and guests of the village in a small basement of the local school, became a symbol. People were kept in this room without ventilation, toilets and electricity for 27 days. This is what volunteer Svitlana Baranova from Slavutych recalled, who was forced to stay in the village of Yahidne because of the shelling:

The orcs [Russian soldiers; author's note] would open the door at 7 a.m. for us to go to the toilet. And not always. There were times when we were locked up for two days or more. Old people used to go to the toilet under themselves. And there was nothing to clean it up with, it stank, it dried up… Four buckets were allocated for the rest of us. But it was not enough for more than three hundred people. There were no exhaust hoods in the basement, there was a terrible stench. People could not stand it and died from lack of oxygen.

At the same time, the Russians began executing one man after the other around the village:

One man was shot when he came out wearing camouflage pants. Another did not want to give up his cell phone. The third asked why they are doing this. Another was killed after reading his correspondence with friends about the war. It was just an ordinary correspondence, something each of us wrote to our relatives and friends.

Hostages in the basement of a school in Yagodnoye, March 2022. (Olga Menyalo via M. Zhirohov)

A 26-year-old local resident of the village recalled:

> Several men were killed, including two brothers, who were found to be helping the Ukrainian Army. One man was tied to a tree and sat blindfolded for a long time. Later we found his grave behind the school. And all because they saw his correspondence with his godfather, who was defending Chernihiv. One guy was killed because he came out to them and asked why they came here, and then shouted, "Glory to Ukraine!" Later, bodies were found in cellars and cars in the village. It is not known how many people died. But at least 20. For a village of 400 people, this is a lot.[2]

There were victims in other communities as well. During the occupation of the Mykhailo-Kotsiubynsk territorial community, eight people were killed – five of them were shot by the Russian military – and, officially, seven were killed in the village of Ivanivka near Chernihiv.

It is worth noting that during the entire period of hostilities, civilians continued to try to leave Chernihiv in the direction of Kyiv at their own risk and, of course, ended up in the area of active hostilities. For example, on 7 March, a car carrying three adults and three children hit an anti-tank mine on the Kyiv highway near the village of Kolychivka. All the adults died on the spot, and the children were taken to hospitals with injuries of varying severity. Eyewitnesses reported that the mines on the road were camouflaged by straw and garbage.

On the same day, a car driven by a 75-year-old resident on the way to chemo dialysis from the Kuvechychi to Chernihiv, was fired upon by BM-27s, while underway on the 01 Highway in the Bilous area. The man burned to death in the car. His wife was with him and escaped. On 9 March, at about 12:00, while trying to leave Chernihiv near the village of Kolychivka, Russian occupants fired at a civilian car, resulting in two deaths and two injuries.

On 12 March, two civilians were killed in the village of Kreschatove, Kozelets district, as a result of rocketing by BM-21s, while several agricultural buildings and one non-residential building were destroyed, and houses and other buildings of about 15 families were damaged. A day later, a minibus moving from the village of Kolychivka in the Kulykivka direction, carrying four people, was hit by a shell. The vehicle burned out, two people were injured and two died.

On the contrary, there is virtually no information about Russian casualties: Moscow imposed strict military censorship and only a few obituaries were made public. The few captured official documents do not enable more than only a rather rough assumption. For example, judging by the 'Report of the Chief of Staff of the 35th Motor Rifle Brigade on the Situation at 11:30 on March 13, 2022', the brigade comprised 1,628 officers and other ranks (amongst them 219 officers): between 24 February and 13 March, it lost 15 killed, 50 wounded, and five captured. In another report based on exchanges in the Russian social media, an element of the same Russian brigade was reported to have lost 132 out of 150 soldiers killed.[3] Additionally, the 35th MRB is known to have lost 31 armoured vehicles, including 10 BMP-1s, 11 T-72s, nine 2S19 Msta-S self-propelled 152mm howitzers, and one radio-communication vehicle.

General Nikolyuk, assessed the enemy's losses as follows:

> According to military practice, if a unit's losses amount to 60 percent, then such a unit should be withdrawn from the battlefield for resupply and restoration of combat capabilities. After our meeting in the Chernihiv forests, the occupiers lost exactly 50% of the total number. And add to the total losses to panic and demoralisation of the personnel in their ranks. If we take these factors into account, the losses of the enemy amounted to 85-90%.[4]

During the Battle of Chernihiv, the Ukrainian defenders are known to have claimed 10 Russian fighter jets, one cruise missile, and one Orlan-10 reconnaissance UAV as shot down. However, with few exceptions – all mentioned above – it proved next to impossible for them to reach the crash sites and inspect the wreckage, and thus relatively little of this was confirmed by visual evidence.

On the contrary, Ukrainian official sources have revealed at least some of the losses of their own armed services. According to the Chernihiv Regional Prosecutor's Office, at least 123 soldiers, 100 civilians, and five police officers had been killed between 24 February and 15 March.[5] The author's own records for the complete duration

A civilian van shot-up by Russians on the way to Chernihiv, March 2022. (Author's collection)

of the battle, are provided in Table 6: they include precise figures for the 119th Independent Brigade of the Territorial Defence, which is known to have lost 73 servicemen killed, and 202 wounded. In turn, its members were credited with the destruction of four T-72s, one ATGM team, one radar, one Su-25 fighter-bomber, two trucks with ammunition, and 28 personnel.

What is also known is that by the end of the siege of Chernihiv, more than half of the city's population of nearly 300,000 had been evacuated. Mayor Vladyslav Atroshenko subsequently estimated the number of civilian victims as 350–400 killed, but also observed that on certain days up to 100 had been buried. Humanitarian workers have claimed similar numbers.[6]

Table 6: ZSU Losses in the Battle of Chernihiv, 24 February – 24 July 2022[7]

	Combat		Other dead	Total
	KIA	WIA		
Armed Forces Of Ukraine	127	1	15	143
Other military formations and law enforcement agencies	32	-	3	35
National Guard of Ukraine	4	-	-	4
DSSU	28	-	3	31
Total	191	1	21	213

In Russian Captivity

'Maxim', a soldier from the 58th Brigade, was captured during the Russian assault on Lukashivka, on 9 March 2022. He recalled:

> My platoon, together with a battalion of Territorial Defence, was in the Chernihiv region. On 9 March, the Russian troops entered the village of Lukashivka and started firing at us from tanks. We fought back as best they could. I was wounded in both legs, hit [in] the thigh, a bullet hit the hand.

Judging by his story, he was taken to a farm and provided with first aid. In pain, he fainted and recovered only the next day, finding himself accompanied by a wounded soldier from the 21st Battalion. Uncertain what was going on outside, the two decided to leave the farm:

> We went to the nearest house. There was a woman in the yard, but she did not allow us to stay there. Russian soldiers went from house to house and intimidated locals if they found them of the Ukrainian military, they pelt[ed] the house with grenades, and those who hid [them] were shot.

Eventually, the woman pointed them at an abandoned building nearby, and they tried to take cover there. While Maxim managed to gather his strength and climb inside through a window, the soldier from the 21st Battalion was caught. Left on his own, Maxim continued hiding for several days. Cold and having no food or water, he was forced to drink his own urine to survive, and to use the same to clean his wounds: 'Meanwhile, the Russians ran out of food and began to loot. They rummaged through the houses in search of food, and they found me. I was dehydrated, I had no strength left to resist. I was blindfolded and tied up [in] some shed I spent the night there'.

The next day, Maxim was transferred to Ivanovka, to the HQ of the 74th GMRB's battalion tactical group. Soon, he was accompanied by two other captured Ukrainians. While there, all the medical aid he received was for the Russians to bandage his wounded hand:

> Then they brought me to their headquarters. There was a lot of Russian special forces there and they began interrogating me. On my hand there was a through wound, they stuck an iron rod in it, and I was beaten everywhere they could reach. They were very interested in where the Ukrainians are hiding American weapons, and demanded me to reveal the position of the Foreign Legion, the foreign volunteers fighting for Ukraine.

During one of the interrogations, a Russian soldier lied to Maxim that they had come from the Omsk region:

> They were angry that we didn't give up. Their commanders told them we would welcome them, that there is no army in Ukraine, and that the people are oppressed. For them, we are fascists, because we chose our own path, and not that of Russia. Russian soldiers had lots of fun that we were captured and they could mock us.

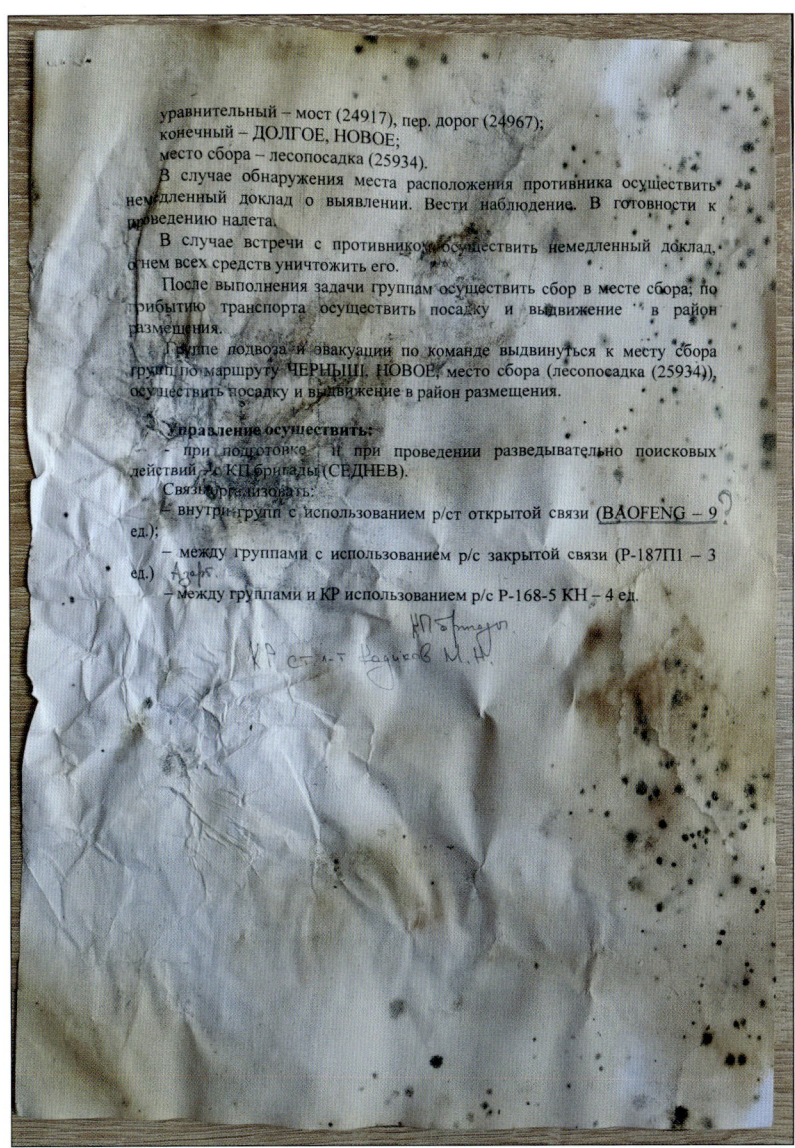

Trophies in the form of captured Russian documents. (Author's collection)

Maxim remained in this place for four days: then, he and other prisoners were put into cars and taken to the border with the Russian Federation, and from there to a major camp for prisoners of war:

> We were brought to a tent city, which was fenced with barbed wire. There were tents everywhere. It was in some city. The soldier who was with me in the tent told that we are somewhere 60 kilometres from the border with the Sumy Oblast. I spent the night there.

The next morning, 16 prisoners, including Maxim, were taken to Kursk:

> We were brought to the Pre-Trial Detention Centre 1. It was like an ordinary prison. In the first cell, I was held together with 22 others. Then they moved some of us to another cell, with only 12. We were all issued black t-shirts and pants. We were not allowed to [sit] on the bed: only on a low bench. Toilet and washing basin were in the middle. Each cell had a camera for video surveillance. And all the time someone near the camera was watching. Every day from 06.00 to 22.00hrs they were playing Russian patriotic songs from the 1940s. We were also forced to learn these songs and sing the anthem of the Russian Federation.

Military and civilians were held together in the cells. Maksym says that civilians were treated like military:

> The Russians did not care to distinguish civilians from military personnel. They called all the captured civilians "fire adjusters" and attributed diverse crimes to them. There were civilians from Kyiv, Zhytomyr, Sumy, and Chernihiv. Also two guys from the Donetsk region…

Torture continued in the Pre-Detention Centre 1 as well:

> As soon as they brought us to the Pre-Trial Detention Centre, they immediately informed us: "You are nobody here, nobody knows about you, we will decide your fate". When they were bored, they took someone out of the cell and practiced theirs blows on them. They beat with us with mops and boards. They also had a kind of guillotine for cutting fingers. They removed someone's internal organs, two were tortured to death.

No international organisations were allowed to visit the prisoners, nor any journalists. 'Investigators' recorded many interrogations on cameras, especially when forcing captives to utter propaganda slogans: resulting recordings were then shown on Russian TV:

> The way they treat us was checked by their own prosecutor, supposedly a human rights commissioner. Before he was to come we were warned how we should behave, what to say. When he came, he asked: "Is everything suits us?", "Are we well fed?", "Are they providing proper medical care?". And we always had to answer: "Yes, of course". If someone tried to answer something else [he] was later hit with a shocker.

All prisoners in the Pre-Trial Detention Centre underwent fluoroscopy, they took a blood test from the finger, took fingerprints. Maxim was seriously wounded, but only on the fifth day of his stay in Kursk was he provided with any kind of 'medical aid':

> They removed the old bandage, nothing was washed, the wound had already started to fester. Applied some ointment and bandaged. Repeated this one procedure every three days.

Due to the lack of proper medical care Maxim's infection began. He was transferred to the hospital, where they were watched by the military police. One day he was simply brought to the prison, they said to prepare for exchange. Eight hours later he and five other soldiers were put on an aircraft, which made another landing somewhere on the territory of the Russian Federation for refuelling. At the same time, several more prisoners were placed with him. The next stop was in the occupied Crimea. Once there, all the prisoners were put in KAMAZ truck and taken to the Zaporizhzhia region:

> At first they let the wounded go and told them to go straight. When we reached our own, I saw Russian prisoners. All of them healthy, without signs of beating. Unlike us. I was immediately taken to the hospital. They provided everything medical assistance as needed.

Conclusions

To summarise the course of hostilities in the Siverskiy region in the spring of 2022, notable was the poor organisation of VSRF units, the unsatisfactory state of its equipment, lack of logistics, and massive violations of the laws of war. Their actions resulted in significant civilian casualties, the creation of a large number of temporarily displaced persons, large material losses, and massive destruction of residential, public and industrial buildings, transport, energy, and utility infrastructure. During the retreat, Russian troops massively and deliberately destroyed residential buildings and social facilities, carried out massive mine-laying, and destroyed bridges and overpasses not justified by tactical necessity. There were massive numbers of murders, robberies, looting, rape and other abuses against the civilian population.

The actions of the Ukrainian troops were generally characterized by determination, a combination of resilience and active defence, an effort to constantly fight to seize and retain the initiative, a desire to achieve tactical success and develop it into operational success, a high level of interaction between various components of the defence forces, types and branches of the armed forces, and non-standard tactical decisions. All of this led to the successful conduct of the defence operation in Chernihiv Oblast, inflicting massive losses to the superior enemy forces, disrupting Putin's plan at the strategic level, and all the planning by his field commanders at operational and tactical levels, and, eventually, forcing the Russians to withdraw because of their inability to restore the combat capability of the involved units.

BIBLIOGRAPHY

Ukrainian language sources are denoted by (UA), Polish (PL), Russian (RU), Czech (CZ).

Books

Bura, D., *Chernihiv: Quadrangle of Unity* (Kharkiv: Folio, 2023) (UA)

Chepurnyj, V., *One hundred days of the Broad War* (Chernihiv: Desna, 2022) (UA)

Collective, *The struggle of the eternal: a chronicle of war and the atrocities of the Russian occupiers in Chernihiv region* (Kyiv: Dakor, 2023) (UA)

Collective, *Unconquered Chernihiv Oblast: Real Stories of the War* (Kyiv: Dakor, 2022) (UA)

Dzyuba S., Puchynecz M., Nazarenko V., Vojtok G., *Chernihiv is on Fire* (Chernihiv: Desna Poligraf, 2022) (UA)

Dzyuba S., Puchynecz M., Nazarenko V., Vojtok G., *Chernihiv is on Fire, Volume 2* (Chernihiv: Desna Poligraf, 2023) (UA)

Gorbulin V., Badrak V., *Above the Abyss: 200 days of the Russian war* (Kyiv: Brait Buks, 2023)

Kharuk A., Zhirokhov M., *Battle chronicle of 2022* (Kyiv: RACIO, 2024) (UA)

Kuxaruk O., *Chernihiv Bastion: Essay on the Great War* (Chernihiv, Desna, 2023) (UA)

Lazun O., *Diary of my war* (Chernihiv, 2023) (UA)

Piotr Szymaniec, Andrzej Małkiewicz, *Wojna nowego wieku? Agresja Rosji przeciw Ukrainie 2022 – 2023* (Inforteditions, 2023) (PL)

Zhirokhov, M., *Northern Outpost: Chernihiv Direction, 2022* (Chernihiv, 2022) (UA)

Zhirokhov, M., *Shield of the North* (Chernihiv, 2023) (UA)

Zhirokhov, M., *Vygovtsi in the Battles for Severshchyna* (Chernihiv, 2022) (UA)

Articles

Fiszer J. & Gruszczyński J., 'Ukraina w ogniu: Obrona powietrzna I lotnictwo', *Lotnictwo Aviation International*, № 4, 2022, pp.10–21. (PL)

Fojtik J., 'Ruské vrtulníky při okupaci Ukrajiny', *ATM*, № 4, 2022, pp.14–15. (CZ)

Gawęda M., 'Wojna rosyjsko-ukraińska. Cz. 1', *Wojsko i Technika*, № 3, 2022, pp.16–24. (PL)

Ripley T., 'Enabling Aggression', *AirForces Monthly*, May 2022, pp.44–49.

Rovenský D., 'Putinova "specoperace": Ruska invaze na Ukrajinu v detailech', *ATM*, April 2022, pp.2–12 (CZ)

Strembski M., 'Wojna powietrzna nad Ukrainą. 24 luty – 23 marca 2022', *Lotnictwo*, № 3, 2022, pp.16–31 (PL)

Trendafilovski V., 'Facing a Blitz', *AirForces Monthly*, № 3, 2022, pp.36–38

Documentary films

Suspilne-Chernihiv, *Battle for Chernihiv* (youtube.com) (UA)

Suspilne-Chernihiv, *Fierce resistance: Pryluki* (youtube.com) (UA)

Suspilne-Chernihiv, *Slavutych is Ukraine* (youtube.com) (UA)

ENDNOTES

Introduction

1   On 8 February 2024, Volodymyr Zelensky by his decree dismissed General Valery Zaluzhny and appointed Colonel General Oleksandr Sirsky to his post. The following day he dismissed Sergey Shaptala, the Chief of the General Staff of the Armed Forces of Ukraine (ZSU). On 7 March 2024, the President of Ukraine Volodymyr Zelenskyy approved the candidacy of Valery Zaluzhny for the post of Ambassador Extraordinary and Plenipotentiary of Ukraine to the United Kingdom of Great Britain and Northern Ireland. The Ministry of Foreign Affairs of Ukraine sent the British side a corresponding request for an agreement, which is one of the preliminary stages of the process of appointing the head of a diplomatic mission. On 19 April 2024, the mass media reported that Zaluzhnyi had received approval (*agrément*) from Britain for the appointment to the post of ambassador. On 8 May 2024, he was discharged from military service on health grounds with the right to wear a military uniform.

Chapter 1

1   Основний бойовий танк Т-64БМ «Булат». URL: https://mil.in.ua/uk/articles/osnovnyj-bojovyj-tank-t-64bm-bulat [August 26, 2009] (UA)

2   David Axe "Ukraine's Best Tank Brigade Has Won The Battle For Chernihiv". URL: https://www.forbes.com/sites/davidaxe/2022/03/31/ukraines-best-tank-brigade-has-won-the-battle-for-chernihiv [March 31, 2022]

3   1st Separate Tank Brigade ORBAT. URL: https://sirdo.substack.com/p/1st-separate-tank-brigade [October 11, 2023]

4   58th Motorized Brigade. URL: https://militaryland.net/ukraine/armed-forces/58th-motorized-brigade [May 9, 2024]

5   У Гончарівську створюють 12-й окремий танковий батальйон. URL: https://www.youtube.com/watch?v=cbZ9qKq-zeE [June 24, 2019] (UA)

6   Регіональному центру радіоелектронної розвідки «Північ» – 26 років. URL: https://www.youtube.com/watch?v=-n121WyR4Nc [December 1, 2017] (UA)

7   У 5-му полку зв'язку відзначили День зв'язківця. URL: https://www.youtube.com/watch?v=AX43EK_5Qv0&t=1s [August 8, 2016] (UA)

8   105 прикордонний загін імені князя Володимира Великого (м. Чернігів). URL: https://dpsu.gov.ua/ua/structure/chastini-centralnogo-pidporyadkuvannya/Chernihivskiy-prikordonniy-zagin (UA)

9   Взвод № 1. НВ називає 25 найвпливовіших українських військових. URL: https://nv.ua/ukr/ukraine/events/generali-peremogi-nv-nazivaye-25-nayvplivovishih-ukrajinskih-viyskovih-50276584.html [October 14, 2022] (UA)

10 During the Battle of Chernihiv, on 10 March 2022, Nikoliuk was awarded the title Hero of Ukraine with the Gold Star. A year later, in March 2023, he was appointed the commander of the Land Forces Training Command, ZSU, but in March 2024, he announced his resignation from that position, and the decision to command a manoeuvre unit on the frontline.

11 After the Battle of Chernihiv, in May 2022, Bryzhinsky was appointed the CO 58th (Independent) Motor Infantry Brigade. In

October 2022, he assumed the position of the Head of Patronage Service of the Chernihiv Oblast, while in February 2023, he was appointed to command the city's military administration. Bryzhinsky was decorated with the Order of Bohdan Khmelnytskyi II and II Degree (on 16 April 2022, and 17 May 2019), Order of Courage Third Degree (14 March 2022), and on 21 September 2022, received the title, 'Honorary Citizen of the City of Chernihiv'.

12 Despite the failures of forces under his command, Lapin retained the command of the OSK Centre until 29 October 2022. Indeed, he was dismissed from that position only following catastrophic Russian losses during the Second Battle of Lyman, and after being fiercely criticised by the Head of the Chechen Republic, Ramazan Kadyrov, who blamed him for a shameful retreat and demanded Lapin to be stripped off all ranks and decorations. For details, see Sam Clench, 'Russia-Ukraine War: General Alexander Lapin removed from Command, Months after Putin called him a Hero', Nzherald.co.nz, 6 November 2022.

Chapter 3

1 Leonid Khoda was born on 29 August 1975. Until 2020 he was deputy commander of the 128th Separate Mountain and Assault Transcarpathian Brigade. From 19 September 2020 he was commander of the 1st Separate Tank "Severskay" Brigade. For personal courage and heroism, demonstrated in the defence of the state sovereignty and territorial integrity of Ukraine, fidelity to the Military Oath by Presidential Decree of Ukraine No. 122/2022 dated 10 March 2022 he was awarded the title of Hero of Ukraine with the presentation of an order "Gold Star".

2 Першими зустріли ворога: у Чернігові привітали з професійним святом прикордонників. URL: https://www.youtube.com/watch?v=jSzuXuyKyks [April 28, 2023] (UA). On 28 March 2022, Chornyi was awarded the Order of Bohdan Khemlnytsyki III Degree for courage in combat.

3 Бойовий комбриг замість мера Чернігова: інтерв'ю Дмитра Брижинського про війну й оборону, роботу в МВА, комерційні оборудки міськради і трагедію в театрі. URL: https://novynarnia.com/2023/10/18/bryzhynskyj-v-Chernihivi [October 18, 2023] (UA)

4 Перші прийняли удар росіян: як згадують події 24 лютого прикордонники з Дніпровського. URL: https://www.youtube.com/watch?v=fjtLsrNYDsA [June 3, 2022] (UA)

5 «Стіна падає на моїх очах, починається пожежа!» – розмова з очевидцем подій на Ніжинському аеродромі URL: https://mynizhyn.com/news/misto-i-region/24624-stina-padae-na-moyih-ochah-pochinaetsja-pozhezha-rozmova-z-ochevidcem-podii-na-nizhinskomu-aerodromi.html [August 17, 2022] (UA)

6 According to Kyiv, between 24 February and 3 May 2022, Russia deployed no fewer than 631 missiles from Belarus. Notably, through early March, and in reaction to pressure from the West, the Russians were deploying their missiles from Belarus by night, or under heavy cloud cover only – apparently in attempt to conceal the flight routes of their weapons. The high point of this campaign was recorded on 9 March, when 35 Iskanders were fired from Belarus at Ukraine. On 1 April, while covering the withdrawal of the VSRF from the Kyiv area, the Russians targeted Ukraine with a total of 56 missiles: about 50 percent of these were OTR-21 Tochka (ASCC/NATO reporting name 'SS-21 Scarab'), fired from the Russian-occupied Donbas. З Білорусі по Україні за час війни російські війська випустили понад 630 ракет. URL: https://suspilne.media/235937-z-bilorusi-po-ukraini-za-cas-vijni-rosijski-vijska-vipustili-ponad-630-raket [May 4, 2022] (UA)

Chapter 4

1 The Russian prisoner of war, Alexander Nikolaevich Bondarenko from the 74th GMRB, was then taken to Chernihiv. His driver-mechanic, Danyil Valeryevich Aminev, was wounded but crawled to the nearby dachas, where the locals hid him until April 2022, when he was handed over to the police. The third crew-member of the destroyed tank, Corporal Alexey Dmitrievich Popov, was killed.

2 Dmytro Kashchenko was born on 24 August 1980 in the Dnipropetrovsk region. In 2001 he graduated from the Kharkiv Institute of Tank Troops with honours. After graduation, he was sent to serve in the 87th Tank Regiment of the 93rd Mechanised Division. He served in the following positions: platoon commander, company commander, chief-of-staff – first deputy battalion commander, commander battalion. Took part in battles in Donbas in 2014–2015 as the commander of the tank battalion of the 93rd Separate Mechanised Brigade. On October 21, 2014, during the preparation for the departure of the convoy of the 79th Separate Airborne Assault Brigade to Donetsk airport for rotation, Lieutenant Colonel Dmytro Kashchenko suffered a second severe wound. He was evacuated first to the military hospital in Dnipro and later transferred to the 2nd Neurological Department of the hospital Mechnikova. In September 2015, he entered the National University of Defence of Ukraine named after Ivan Chernyakhovsky, from which he graduated in March 2017. He was appointed deputy commander of the 17th Separate Tank Brigade. From September 2019, he was the commander of the 58th Separate Motorized Infantry Brigade. On 15 April 2022, in his daily address, the President of Ukraine, Volodymyr Zelenskyi, reported on conferring the title of Hero of Ukraine on Dmytro Kashchenko a personal example of heroism that inspired comrades on duty, for extremely effective combat operations and concrete and very important results for the preservation of the positions of our army and the expulsion of the occupiers.

3 He served in the Soviet Army. As a volunteer in the paramilitary "Right Sector", he worked as a sapper in engineering support in the Donetsk direction – Kurakhivka, Krasnohorivka, Savur-Mohyla, Stepanivka, Pisky, Donetsk airport. Since 2015, he served as part of the 250th Engineering Support Centre. As of February 2022, he was the deputy unit commander and the chief engineer. On March 26, 2022, he was awarded the title "Hero of Ukraine".

4 N. Shcherbina, *'Tankist "Mars": "Mi visunulisya 3 tankami proti 30 vzvod proti batalyonu"'*, Cheline (11 Sep 2022).

5 Major Shchetkin was quickly exchanged, but Senior Sergeant Kulikov was tried in August 2022 and sentenced to 10 years in prison and procedural costs of 26,000 hryvnias for violating the laws and customs of war (the court proved that a tank had fired at a residential building along the convoy). Kulikov was exchanged in June 2023.

6 «Тату, все буде добре». Останній бій Івана Коваля з Городнянщини. URL: https://susidy.city/articles/226264/tatu-vse-bude-dobre-ostannij-bij-ivana-kovalya-z-gorodnyanschini [July 27, 2022] (UA)

Chapter 5

1 Герой України Віктор Ніколюк: це Збройні Сили змусили росіян відійти від Чернігова. URL: https://suspilne.media/chernihiv/224112-geroj-ukraini-viktor-nikoluk-ce-zbrojni-sili-zmusili-rosian-vidijti-vid-cernigova [April 1, 2022] (UA)

2 Врятували Чернігів від оточення: спогади українських військових про бій у Количівці URL: https://suspilne.media/chernihiv/274611-vratuvali-cernigiv-vid-otocenna-spogadi-ukrainskih-vijskovih-pro-bij-u-kolicivci [August 24, 2022] (UA)

3 This description of the battle of Kolychikva is based on Suspilne-Chernihiv, 'The encirclement of Chernihiv…', YouTube, 30 May 2022, and Aleksandr Shulman, 'Батальйон «виговців» за місяць затрофеїв 10 танків росії', *ArmyInform.com.ua*, 18 May 2022.

4 7 разів возили на розстріл. Як вербували росіяни. Чому сидів у найжорсткішій українській колонії. URL: https://www.youtube.com/watch?v=DWGqwuaEw64 [June 4, 2024] (UA)

5 Висота. Як українські бійці зупинили росіян під Черніговом URL: https://texty.org.ua/projects/109122/vysota-yak-ukrayinski-bijci-zupynyly-rosiyan-pid-chernihovom (UA)

Chapter 6

1 Війна в Україні: яких руйнувань зазнав Чернігів. URL: https://chernihivnews.city/articles/196874/shist-dniv-vijni-yakih-rujnuvan-zaznav-Chernihiv- [March 2, 2022] (UA)

2 Авіаудар по Чернігову, де загинули 47 людей, можна розцінювати як військовий злочин. URL: https://suspilne.media/chernihiv/215618-aviaudar-po-cernigovu-de-zaginuli-47-ludej-mozna-rozcinuvati-ak-vijskovij-zlocin [March 9, 2022] (UA)

3 Легендарна історія – як взяли в полон пілота, який бомбардував Чернігів. URL: https://www.youtube.com/watch?v=70kWVfN678M [March 23, 2024] (UA) & Суд не

пом'якшив вирок російському льотчику Красноярцеву, який бомбардував Чернігів у лютому-березні 2022 року. URL: https://www.youtube.com/watch?v=XSLAqiv3_cs [January 22, 2024] (UA). On 18 April 2022, Major Krasonyartsev was exchanged for a Ukrainian pilot. On 26 October 2023, he was then sentenced by the Novozavodsk District Court of Chernihiv, in absentia, to 14 years in prison and two million Ukrainian Hryna of compensation for the damage he caused. The Border Guards that shot him down were awarded the Defender of the Fatherland medal on 16 March 2022.

4   Eight days later, on 13 March 2022, the successful MANPAD operator was decorated with the Order of Bohdan Khmelnytsky, III Degree.

5   Тіло збитого під Черніговом російського льотчика повернули додому через чотири місяці. URL: https://www.unian.ua/war/viyna-proti-rosiji-tilo-zbitogo-pid-Chernihivom-rosiyskogo-lotchika-povernuli-dodomu-cherez-chotiri-misyaci-novini-vtorgnennya-rosiji-v-ukrajinu-11881098.html [June 27, 2022] (UA). Gatarov was a native of Chelyabinsk Oblast. His body was returned to Russia in June 2022. He was buried in the village of Khalitovo, in Kunashak district. Runov's helmet was saved as a war trophy in the Chernihiv Historical Museum V Tarnovsky.

6   Окупанти з РФ розбомбили стадіон чернігвської «Десни» і музей. URL: https://www.pravda.com.ua/news/2022/03/11/7330317 [March 11, 2022] (UA)

7   Меморіал пам'яті: військовий льотчик Володимир Скляр. URL: https://chernihiv.today/memorial-pam-jati-vijskovij-lotchik-volodimir-skljar [February 11, 2023] (UA). Chyzh and Pepelashko were held captive in the Kursk Detention Centre, along with other captured Ukrainian soldiers. On 14 April 2022, they were exchanged for Major Krasnoyartsev.

8   Як сержант ЗСУ збив ворожий літак у небі над Черніговом. URL: https://www.sknews.net/yak-serzhant-zsu-zbyv-vorozhyy-litak-u-nebi-nad-chernihovom [January 16, 2023] (UA)

9   «Відкриваю очі: люди лежать»: розповідають ті, хто вижив після обстрілу черги за хлібом. URL: https://mipl.org.ua/vidkryvayu-ochi-lyudy-lezhat-rozpovidayut-ti-hto-vyzhyv-pislya-obstrilu-chergy-za-hlibom [June 6, 2022] (UA); Amnesty International, 'Ukraine: Russian 'Dumb Bomb' Air Strike killed Civilians in Chernihiv – New Investigation and Testimony', 9 March 2022; Humans Rights Watch, 'Ukraine: Russian Strikes killed Scored of Civilians in Chernihiv', 10 June 2022; Ukrinform, 'Ворог накрив артилерією Чернігів, серед загиблих – американець', 17 March 2022.

10 Воєнні злочини на Чернігівщині: короткий огляд за результатами моніторингових виїздів із документування. URL: https://lb.ua/blog/koalitsiia_ua5am/557680_voienni_zlochini_Chernihivshchini.html [May 29, 2023] (UA)

11 В центрі Чернігова вночі через обстріли горів ринок та торговий центр. URL: https://suspilne.media/chernihiv/223118-v-centri-cernigova-vnoci-cerez-obstrili-goriv-rinok-ta-torgovij-centr [March 30, 2022] (UA)

Chapter 7

1   Russians start to withdraw from Chernobyl: US. URL: https://www.france24.com/en/live-news/20220330-russians-start-to-withdraw-from-chernobyl-us [March 30, 2022]

2   Захисник ЧАЕС Артем Лутченко, який схуд у полоні на 24 кілограми, мріє про вінчання і дітей. URL: https://24tv.ua/obmin-polonenimi-31-travnya-yaki-plani-zhittya-natsgvardiytsya_n2568876 [June 4, 2024] (UA)

3   Друга річниця окупації Славутича: спогади містян, як усе відбувалося. URL: https://podrobnosti.ua/2478056-druga-rchnitsja-okupats-slavuticha-spogadi-mstjan-jak-use-vdbuvalosja.html [March 26, 2024] (UA)

Chapter 8

1   Цистерни з Корюківщини, на які місцеві навели вогонь українських військових, тимчасово передали "Укрзалізниці". URL: https://suspilne.media/chernihiv/330104-cisterni-z-korukivsini-na-aki-miscevi-naveli-vogon-ukrainskih-vijskovih-timcasovo-peredali-ukrzaliznici [December 2, 2022] (UA)

2   Координатор Руху Опору з Чернігівщини про розвідку, найчастіші помилки та мотивацію. URL: https://www.youtube.com/watch?v=54nDQEnGo8s [June 5, 2024] (UA)

Chapter 10

1   На Чернігівщині під час бойових дій загинуло 432 цивільні особи. URL: https://pravda.cn.ua/na-Chernihivshini-pid-chas-boiovih-dii-zaginylo-432-civilni-osobi [April 26, 2022] (UA)

2   Страшні й безжальні історії окупації. Як мати з Ягідного втратила двох синів. URL: https://vikna.tv/istorii/strashni-j-bezzhalni-istoriyi-okupacziyi-yak-maty-z-yagidnogo-vtratyla-dvoh-syniv [June 12, 2022] (UA)

3   Ilia Ponomarenko, 'EXCLUSIVE: Voice Message reveals Russian Military Unit's catastrophic Losses in Ukraine', Kyiv Independent, 2 March 2022.

4   Як здійснювалася оборона «Північного форпосту» від рашистських загарбників. URL: https://armyinform.com.ua/2023/03/22/yak-zdijsnyuvalasya-oborona-pivnichnogo-forpostu-vid-rashystskyh-zagarbnykiv/?utm_source=mainnews&utm_medium=article&utm_campaign=traficsource [March 22, 2023] (UA)

5   'Щонайменше 123 військових та 100 цивільних загинули на Чернігівщині з початку вторгнення РФ', Supline.media, 15 April 2022.

6   Max Bearak & Siobhan O'Grady, 'In shattered Chernihiv, Russian Siege leaves a City asking, "Why?"', The Washington Post, 10 April 2022.

7   Calculated by the author based on materials from his own archive.

ABOUT THE AUTHOR

Mykhailo Zhyrokhov was born in the Donetsk region of Ukraine in 1974. He works as professional historian, specialised in conflicts in the post-Soviet countries and military aviation. He has written an impressive number of books published in Russian, Ukrainian, English and French, and has attended numerous conferences relating to the Russian–Ukrainian war fought since 2014. He currently heads the Chernihiv Military History Museum.